Abstracts of Early EAST TEXAS Newspapers,

1839-1856

Compiled By:
Linda Cheves Nicklas

Copyright 1994
By: Southern Historical Press, Inc.

All rights reserved. No part of this publication may be reproduced,
stored in a retrieval system, transmitted in any form,
posted on to the web in any form or by any means
without the prior written permission of the publisher.

Please direct all correspondence and orders to:

www.southernhistoricalpress.com
or
SOUTHERN HISTORICAL PRESS, Inc.
PO BOX 1267
375 West Broad Street
Greenville, SC   29601
southernhistoricalpress@gmail.com

ISBN #0-89308-503-0

Printed in the United States of America

Introduction

The inspiration for this publication came when I discovered in some papers deposited in Steen Library, abstracts from early issues of <u>The Standard</u>, <u>The Northern Standard</u>, and <u>The Red-Lander</u> newspapers. A staff member had painstakingly read the papers, apparently in the 1950s, on the much poorer quality microfilm readers then available and abstracted articles of local interest. I decided to expand and build on that work by abstracting articles from other East Texas newspapers with the goal of putting all the material together in book form.

Newspapers abstracted include:

Clarksville	<u>The Northern Standard</u>, 1842-1853
Clarksville	<u>The Standard</u>, 1853-1856
Marshall	<u>The Texas Republican</u>, 1849-1852
Nacogdoches	<u>Nacogdoches Times</u>, 1848-1849
Nacogdoches	<u>Nacogdoches Chronicle</u>, 1852-1855
San Augustine	<u>The Red-Lander</u>, 1839-1846, 1854
San Augustine	<u>The Journal and Advertiser</u>, 1840-1841

A few issues of other Texas newspapers which contain articles relating to East Texas were also included.

Articles of historical interest, such as those on the establishment of new towns and steamship travel, as well as marriage and death notices are abstracted. Because the state did not require the filing of death cerificates until 1903, it is sometimes difficult, if not impossible, to locate information on early- and mid-nineteenth century deaths. This publication will help to fill that void. Many marriage notices are included even though they may appear in county records, because the newspaper notices often gave additional information not available elsewhere, such as parents' names, state of origin, and the full names of the parties. Also, a researcher may not know in which county to look for marriage records. Discrepencies in many published sources prompted me to give the newspaper's interpretation of the spellings of names and the very important use of the title "Mrs."

A number of East Texas counties have suffered devastating losses of records due to courthouse fires. In the cases of "burned " counties, not only were marriages included, but so was other information ordinarily found in county records, such as probate notices. For some especially interesting or short items, the entire article is included, rather than an abstract of it.

Many of the spelling, punctuation, and capitalization usages of the time are retained. Places are included in the index if they are outside of East Texas, if they are now ghost towns or are not well known, or if the information in the text is about the place itself, rather than about an event which occurred there.

In order to finish this project after working on it for almost two years, the decision was made not to re-read the newspapers which were abstracted years ago. Some spot-checking was done, however, and it was discovered that a few very short items were missed entirely, including some death and marriage notices. A number of names were transcribed incorrectly, probably due to the poor quality of the earlier generation microfilm readers. When found, errors were corrected and the correct information included in this publication.

I want to thank my husband, Gunter Nicklas, who spent untold hours entering all the abstracts into our home computer during his spare time and the student assistants in Steen Library for their help, especially with the index. I also appreciate the assistance of Jan Todd Linthicum, who proof-read the finished manuscript, and Marty Weitzel Turnage for lending support and encouragement.

TABLE OF CONTENTS

Introduction.. i-ii
The Red-Lander, 1839-1846, 1854...................... 1-25
Nacogdoches Times, 1848-1849......................... 26-30
Nacogdoches Chronicle, 1852-1855..................... 31-51
The Northern Standard, 1842-1853..................... 52-86
The Standard, 1853-1856.............................. 87-101
The Texas Republican, 1849-1852......................102-117
Journal Advertiser, 1840-1841........................   118
The Texas Union, 1849................................118-120
The Daily Texas, 1842................................   121
The Texas Times, 1842................................   121
Telegraph and Texas Register, 1842...................   121
The Morning Star, 1842...............................   122
Democratic Telegraph and Texas Register, 1850........   122
Index..123-159

THE RED-LANDER, San Augustine, Texas

October 1839

SMITHFIELD

The town of Smithfield is situated on the Coshatta Bluffs, on the east side of the Trinity River, upon a high, healthy Bluff surrounded by a luxuriant country, enjoying plenty of the best spring water; having the advantage of Timber for building purposes, with Saw Mills in the immediate vicinity; about one hundred miles from Galveston, with which place there is water communication by steam boats.

CITY OF SABINE

W. D. Lee, merchant, commission and forwarding, will make liberal advances on consignments of Cotton for shipment either to the United States, or to Europe direct.

NOTICE

The undersigned will attend to the purchase and sale of Texas lands, he is very well acquainted in all Eastern Texas, and has been his residence for the last eleven years, he is well acquainted with the citizens of Eastern Texas. Any business that he may be trusted with, shall be promptly attended to.
                                        W. D. R. Speight

CUSTOM HOUSE

Sabine Pass. All vessels for Sabine River are hereby notified that they are required to entre [sic] before they pass the Custom House, - and any disregarding this notice shall be dealt with to the utmost rigor of the law.
                                        R. C. Doom,
                                        Collector for District Sabine

NOTICE

The undersigned begs leave to inform the citizens of San Augustine and Shelby counties, that he has obtained an appointment as Deputy Surveyor of Nacogdoches county, and will start on the 20th inst. to that delightful part of the country lying between the main Trinidad River, the Cross Timbers and the Bois D'acre fork of the Trinidad. Any persons having lands to locate would do well to give him a call at Shelbyville, as he intends to devote his time and attention to the location of lands. His terms will be reasonable.
                                        C. L. Mann.

THE RED-LANDER, SAN AUGUSTINE

CALHOUN

The proprietors have at length come to the determination to bring this town into notice by giving the public an opportunity of making investments. Situated in the heart of one of the most fertile portions of Eastern Texas, on the west bank of the Angelina, on the great thoroughfare leading from the north-eastern part of Texas to the cities of Houston, Galveston, and Brazoria...

It is nearly equal distant, from the towns of Zavala, Nacogdoches and San Augustine, and is about thirty miles from either place; and is in one of the healthiest portions of Eastern Texas. It abounds with the purest spring water, within the actual limits of the town; immediately adjacent is also one of the finest sulphur springs in the Republic which no doubt contains many medicinal properties. With regard to the navigation of the Angelina with steamboats to Calhoun, at all seasons of the year when they can run in any stream in Texas; It is no longer considered impracticable even by the most sceptical.

Jno. T. Paterson,
Wm. M. Hurt,
Sam'l Needham,
Proprietors.

SHERIFF'S SALE

I will expose at public sale on the first Tuesday in November next, at the court house door in the town of Milam, all the right, title and interest that William B. Harvey has in and to a certain tract of land... to satisfy an execution in my hands in favor of Willis Murphey.
Wm. Earl, Sheriff.

I will expose to public sale on the first Tuesday in November next, at the court house door in the town of Milam, all the right, title and interest that John Davis has in and to a certain tract of land... to satisfy an execution in favor of S. M. Slaughter against John Davis and Samuel Thompson.
Wm. Earl, Sheriff.

ADMINISTRATOR'S NOTICE

All persons indebted to the estate of James Conn, deceased, of Jasper county, are required to make immediate payment, and all having claims against said estate are requested to present them within the time prescribed by law or they will be forever barred. Ruffin Turner, Adm'r.

May 27, 1841

ADMINISTRATRIX NOTICE

Probate Court for the county of Shelby. The estate of Joseph C. Yates, late of said county, dec'd. Elizabeth Yates, Administratrix.

ADMINISTRATOR'S NOTICE

The undersigned having obtained letters of Administration on the estate of Joel Robertson deceased, late of Jasper county.

S. H. Everett, Administrator.

June 10, 1841

ADMINISTRATOR'S NOTICE

The Estates of Palafox and Hanson Hinds, dec'd., by Hon. Probate court in and for the county of Sabine. Homer Hinds, Adm'r.

Probate Court held in Milam, Sabine County, the estate of Moses Speer, deceased. Littleton Fowler, Administrator.

Probate Court held in Milam, Sabine County. Estate of Elizabeth Porter, deceased. Littleton Fowler, Administrator.

July 8, 1841

SHOOTING

A man by the name of Meadows was shot in the town of Milam on Monday last, by Allison A. Lewis of the same county.

July 22, 1841

DIED

In this county on Sunday morning last, Mr. John Cartwright, aged 51 years.

ADMINISTRATOR'S NOTICE

Probate Court of the county of Shelby. The Estate of John Stewart, deceased, late of said county. Lewis Watkins, Admin'r.

THE RED-LANDER, SAN AUGUSTINE

July 29, 1841

DIED

In this county on the 22d inst., Mrs. Anne Holman, aged 58 years.

September 2, 1841

COUNTY OF SHELBY

We are gratified to learn the troubles in Shelby and Harrison counties have been in a great measure quieted, and it is confidently believed that order and harmony will now be permanently established. That such may be the case, is the ardent wish of every friend to his country. The citizens of the adjoining counties have beheld with the deepest regret, the army of hostile parties in their immediate vicinity, and would have interposed their friendly mediation, if they had been acquainted with many of the facts during the time of the excitement.

That Shelby county is yet cursed with many of the old "Tenehaw gang," is doubtless but too true. But there is nothing so effectual, in purging society of the dregs, that are always found in its first formation in new countries, as the steady yet constant influence of a virtuous, discriminating public sentiment. This county was not a whit better than Shelby, three years ago: now she may proudly rank among the first in the Republic. A great and wonderful revolution has been wrought, by the force of public sentiment. A short time since, our community was ruled and held in terror by ruthless vagabonds, loafers and gamblers: Now, their influence is unknown - a regular blackleg is rarely to be found in our county.

September 9, 1841

EDUCATION

The good citizens of Nacogdoches are making some praise- worthy exertions to encourage the business of education, among the rising generation. Many excellent schools are in operation in different parts of the county, and the zeal and ability of some of their preceptors is well worthy the commendation and patronage of parents and guardians.

A committee of gentlemen who attended an examination of the school of Mr. Moffit, have favored us with their correspondence with that gentleman, together with a copy of his address, which we take pleasure in publishing; trusting that it will be read by all who feel an interest in the cause of education, perhaps encourage them to a more vigorous and zealous performance of a duty encumbent on every person who has the future welfare of his country at heart.

ADMINISTRATOR'S NOTICE

At the last term of the Probate Court held in Milam, Sabine County, on Monday the 28th of June the undersigned was appointed by the Court, administrator of the estate of William Wallace, dec'd.

W. M. Earl, Adm'r. of the estate.

NOTICE

In the Probate Court of Houston County,   Clinton A. Price.[Rice?]
[vs.]
The heirs of Rob't Erwin.

The plaintiff, Clinton A. Price, having filed his petition in this Court praying to have his part of the estate of Robert Erwin, dec'd., partitioned, and ... two of the heirs of said estate, are non residents of this country, viz: James McKelvey and James Latham.

September 16, 1841

ADMINISTRATOR'S NOTICE

At the May Term of the Probate Court for Sabine county, letters of Administration were granted to the undersigned on the estates of B. Mulholland and S. R. Collins.

Wm. P. Wyche.

September 23, 1841

DIED

In this city on the 22 inst., Mr. Augustus Phelps, aged 23 years.

October 14, 1841

DOINGS AT THE ALTAR

Married - On the 14th of September, last, in Fort Houston, Col. James Carr, Attorney and counsellor at law, of Houston County, to Mary Myers Hunter, eldest daughter of the late General Nathaniel Smith of Burnet County.

OBITUARY

General Nathaniel Smith is no more - He departed this life on the 17th of September ... near this place, in the 50th year of his age.

THE RED-LANDER, SAN AUGUSTINE

October 21, 1841

MARRIED

In this county, on the 13th inst., Mr. F. Dixon to Mrs. Melissa Hampton, both of this county.

October 28, 1841

MARRIED

In Nacogdoches County, on Thursday evening, the 14th last, Capt. William Bell to Miss Lucinda, daughter of James Walling, Esq., all of the same county.

In the vicinity of Melrose on Friday evening, the 22nd, inst., by the Hon'l Wm. Hart, Dr. T. Jeff Johnson to Miss Amanda Engledow, all of Nacogdoches county.
P.S. To the members of the Marrying Club in San Augustine: Wedding cake is the order of the day about Melrose - and girls are plenty - boys come over!

In Shelbyville, on 21st ult., by the Rev. Wm. Crawford, Dr. Wm. P. Landrum to Mrs. Catharine, relict of the late Wm. B. Hicks.

May 26th, 1842

DIED

In this city, on Monday the 9th inst., after a lingering illness of Tubercular consumption, Mrs. Louise Crane, consort of Mr. P. S. Crane, aged 25 years.

ADMINISTRATOR'S NOTICE

Letters of administration having been granted to the undersigned, on the 18th April 1842, upon the estate of Tandy K. Martin, late of Sabine county...
                                            Mrs. Martin, Admr'x.
                                    Widow of T. K. Martin, dec'd.

July 7th, 1842

OBITUARY

Another Hero of San Jacinto gone. The Hon. Isaac N. Moreland, late Chief Justice of Harris County, and Commander of the Artillery company in the battle of San Jacinto, died in this city on Thursday morning. His remains were followed to the grave by a large and respectable concourse of citizens, including the Masonic and other fraternities, and the independent military companies of the city, and many of his companions in arms, who had stood by him in the field of battle, assembled around the grave, to pay the last tribute of respect to their beloved comrade.- Telegraph.

July 28, 1842

OBITUARY

Departed this life at the residence of Capt. David Augustus in Nacogdoches County, Texas, on the 4th of the present inst., Mr. Nicholas J. Taliaferro, in the 20th year of his age.
Mr. Taliaferro was a native of Madison county, Alabama, and but a few days before his death had returned from a campaign on our Western frontier.

NOTICE

Dr. George S. Hyde, having resumed the practice of medicine, respectfully tenders his professional services to the citizens of Nacogdoches County. Residence Nacogdoches.

October 6, 1842

ADMINISTRATRIX'S NOTICE

Shelby county. Estate of John Beauchamp, deceased.
Susan Beauchamp, Admr'x.

PETITION FOR DIVORCE

County of Shelby. Mason M. Vann vs. Jane Vann.
Whereas, at the said term of said court, it appearing to the satisfaction of the court that the defendant, Jane Vann, resides beyond the limit of said republic ... court will proceed to hear said suit.

October 20, 1842

OBITUARY

Died, at the residence of her father, on the evening of the 10th inst., Miss Francis, eldest daughter of John G. Love, Esqr., of this county.
In the death of this amiable young lady, an aged parent has lost the first tender pledge of Heaven's love, and only earthly object to which he fondly looked to comfort his grey hairs [having recently lost his bosom companion].

THE RED-LANDER, SAN AUGUSTINE

DIED

In Sabine county, on Saturday last, Mr. Charles Morse.

November 10, 1842

ADMINISTRATOR'S NOTICE

County of Shelby. Letters of administration having been granted to the undersigned upon the estate of Charles W. Jackson.
          Matthew Brinson, Administrator.

December 15, 1842

ADMINISTRATRIX' NOTICE

Sabine County. Estate of Robert Oliver, dec'd.
    Nancy Oliver, adm'x.   J. W. Oliver, adm'r.

February 9, 1843

OBITUARY

Died, at the residence of Mr. J.J. Hennise on the 23d January last, Mr. John E. Pennington, aged 49 years. Mr. Pennington was a citizen of Arkansas, where his family are now residing.

February 16, 1843

DIVORCE

Sabine County. Catherine Coleman vs. Alexander Coleman. Whereas, Catherine Coleman hath on 10th of December 1842, filed in the office of the clerk of the District Court in and for the county of Sabine and Republic of Texas her petition for divorce.

DIED

On the 13th inst., Robert Devin, infant son of Wm. M. and Mary L. Hurt, aged 6 months.

DIVORCE

Abigal B. Kendall vs. Alman Kendall.
    County of Sabine. In this case, it appearing to the satisfaction of the court that Alman Kendall is not an

inhabitant of this Republic ...to appear in court and show cause ...why judgement shall not be granted.

March 27, 1843

ADMINISTRATRIX' NOTICE

Houston County. Letters of administration, on the succession of James Brent, dec'd., who died intestate, having been granted to the subscriber. Sarah Brent, Administrator.

DEBT

Shelby County. John D. English vs. Presly E. George. In this case it appearing to the satisfaction of the court, that, the said Presly E. George is not a citizen of the Republic...

April 15, 1843

KILLED

On Monday night the 1st inst., a man named Jefferson Haggerty was killed by the Sheriff's deputy while attempting to escape from custody. Haggerty had been convicted for larceny, and the Sheriff, his deputy, and a guard were escorting him to Jail for safe keeping, when he broke from the custody of the officers and was shot dead.

NOTICE

Shelby County. John M. Bradley, admin. on the estates of Samuel Rasiter [Rositer], Nelson Howel [Howell], Ephraim Stary [Story], Harriet Nail, and Ann Gray.

May 13, 1843

MARRIED

On Sunday evening, 30th April, by Parson Ha... Mr. Nickloss Y. Moore to Miss Eliza Jane, daughter of Doctor Samuel Stivers. All of Nacogdoches county.

ADMINISTRATOR'S NOTICE

County of Jasper. Estate of Nancy Walker, deceased, of Jasper County... A. C. Swearingin, Admin.

THE RED-LANDER, SAN AUGUSTINE

August 5, 1843

$100 REWARD

Whereas, Littleberry B. Franks and Lucius Johnson, who were in my custody, charged with the murder of Henry Casdedine, did on the evening of Monday last, the 10th of July, escaped from the guard during the storm and darkness of the night...
Ordera Watson, Sheriff of Milam County.

NOTICE

County of Jasper. Estate of James A. Winn, dec'd.
Quean Elizabeth Winn, Administratrix.

DIVORCE

County of Sabine. Catherine Coleman vs. Alexander Coleman. In this case it appearing to the satisfaction of the Court that Alexander Coleman the defendant in this case is a non resident of this Republic...

August 12, 1843

ADMINISTRATOR'S NOTICE

Shelby County. The undersigned, having been duly appointed Administrator on the Estate of Matthew Moore...
Gabriel H. Moore, Administrator.

September 2, 1843

DIED

At the residence of his father two miles west of San Augustine, John C. Garrett, the only son of William Garrett, Esqr. Aged 9 years.

September 9, 1843

DIED

In this city, on Monday last, Mr. James Tabor, aged 37 years.

In this county at the residence of Mr. John Nicholson, Widow Mary McIver, aged 77 years.

In Nacogdoches county, on Saturday the 2d inst., Mrs. Sarah M. Eubanks, aged 19 years.

In this city, on Thursday last, Mr. Isaac Campbell, aged 30 years.

DIVORCE

Nacogdoches County. Anderson Webb vs. Ruannear (?) Webb...she being a non-resident of the Republic ... to appear to show why judgement should not be made.

October 14, 1843

PARTITION

Houston County. George W. Browning, Guardian of George Campbell vs. Estate of George Campbell, dec'd... notifying Eton Campbell, one of the heirs of G. C. Campbell, dec'd., a non-resident of the Republic, to appear to show cause.

November 4, 1843

HEIRS OF MARTIN LACY

Houston County. William Y. Lacy, et. al., heirs of Martin Lacy vs. William White, bill for specific performance. William Y. Lacy, William K. Lacy, Hillary R. Lacy, William G. W. Jowers(?) and his wife, Nancy Jowers (?), William Sims and his wife, Mary Sims, and Martha Burton, heirs of Martin Lacy, dec'd., appeal to the court.

SUPPORT

Houston County. Catharine Logan vs. William Logan ... for support ... said William Logan's residence unknown.

November 25, 1843

ACCIDENTAL DEATH

A Mr. Turner, of Bastrop country, was riding out lately with his wife and child. The horse was hooked by an ox and took fright. Mrs. Turner was thrown under a waggon, the wheels of which passed over her body, killing her on the spot. The child had its arm broken.

ADMINISTRATION

Rusk County. Estate of George Birdwell ... letters of administration granted to M. R. Birdwell, Administrator.

THE RED-LANDER, SAN AUGUSTINE

December 16, 1843

ADMINISTRATORS' NOTICE

Houston County. Estate of Geo. Aldrich, deceased, late of said county. Waller, Dickerson, Administrator.

Houston County. Estate of Wm. P. Davis ... J. F. Roberts, Administrator, Sarah Davis, Administratrix.

December 23, 1843

DIED

Yesterday morning at 5 o'clock, at the residence of his brother, 3 miles east of this city, Sandford Holman, aged about 28 years.

January 13, 1844

DIED

In Sabine County, on Friday, Mrs. Martha Renfro, wife of David Renfro--aged about 32 years.

January 20, 1844

PARTITION

Estate of James Brent

Houston County. Lodwich (?) D. Downs and Harriet M., his wife vs. William Hendricks and Elizabeth, his wife, Benjamin N.(?) Butterworth and Margaret M., his wife, James Brent, Alfred Price and Sally Ann, his wife, heirs of James Brent, deceased.... the defendant heirs are not residents of the Republic.

February 24, 1844

OBITUARY

Departed this life on Thursday, the 4th January, in Houston County, Mary Ann, consort of Col. S.L.B. Jasper.... She has paid the great debt of nature, and left a disconsolate husband and three orphan children.

ADMINISTRATOR'S NOTICE

Shelby County. Estate of Samuel Hall, late of said county, deceased ... Amos Hall and James Hall, administrators.

THE RED-LANDER, SAN AUGUSTINE

March 9, 1844

PARTITION

Sabine County. Jefferson W. Oliver vs. Nancy Oliver, Ananias G. Oliver, George W. Oliver, Robert F. Oliver, Robert Portwood, John L. Brown, the heirs of Thos. G. Birdwell. Robert Portwood and John L. Brown are nonresidents of the Republic.

March 23, 1844

ADMINISTRATOR'S NOTICE

Shelby County. Estate of Clement L. Wharton, deceased. Nathan Matthews, Administrator.

Sabine County. Estate of Jefferson Wilson, late of Sabine County. Betty Wilson, Administratrix.

April 6, 1844

ADMINISTRATOR'S NOTICE

Sabine County. Estate of Mrs. Matilda Wall, deceased. Theo. Harris, Administrator.

April 27, 1844

ADMINISTRATOR'S NOTICE

Shelby County. Estate of Abner S. Waller, late of said county, deceased. W. W. Lanier, Administrator.

June 1, 1844

SUCCESSION

Houston County. Estate of Col. Samuel Payne, deceased. R. W. Davis, Administrator.

MARRIED

On Thursday evening May the 30th, by the Rev. L. Jones, Madison H. Shryock, Esq., of Houston to Miss Jane E. Perkins of this county.

THE RED-LANDER, SAN AUGUSTINE

June 8, 1844

DIED

In this city, on the 5th inst., John Calvin, youngest son of Wm. H. and the late Hannah A. G. Slaughter--aged 4 years, 3 months and 14 days.

August 17, 1844

DIVORCE

Sabine County. Joseph R. Bass vs. Catherine Bass. The defendant is a nonresident of the Republic of Texas.

August 24, 1844

DIED

On the 4th instant, at his residence in Nacogdoches, of an old chronic affliction, Mr. Robert LeMaird (?) at the advanced age of sixty seven. Left a large family.

August 31, 1844

ADMINISTRATOR'S NOTICE

Shelby County. Estate of Stephen Holmes, dec'd., late of said county. Thos. B. Davenport, adm'r.

September 21, 1844

ADMINISTRATOR'S NOTICE

Jasper County. Estate of Dr. Stephen H. Everitt, deceased, late of said county. Z. Wm. Eddy, Administrator.

October 19, 1844

OBITUARY

Departed this life, on Sunday evening, the 13th inst., Mr. Louis M. Flatau, merchant of this city (formerly of Berlin, Prussia), aged about 26 years.

October 26, 1844

DIVORCE

Houston County. Daniel E. Harper vs. Elizabeth Harper. The defendant is a nonresident of the Republic of Texas.

THE RED-LANDER, SAN AUGUSTINE

ADMINISTRATOR'S NOTICE

Shelby County. Estate of James Tucker. L. V. Greer, Administrator.

December 7, 1844

ADMINISTRATOR'S NOTICE

Houston County. Estate of Samuel Payne, deceased, late of said county. A. E. McClure, Administrator.

December 28, 1844

ADMINSTRATOR'S NOTICE

Shelby County. Estate of John M. Bradley, deceased, late of said county. Richard Hooper, Administrator.

January 4, 1845

DIED

In this county on the 30th ult., Mary Ann Houston Daniel, daughter of William and Martha Daniel, aged 3 years, 1 month and 9 days.

ADMINISTRATOR'S NOTICE

Shelby County. Estate of John Dial, deceased. Joseph Dial, A. W. O. Hicks, N. G. Dial, W. L. Landrum, Administrators.

February 8, 1845

DIVORCE

Sabine County. Jefferson W. Oliver vs. Sarah J. Oliver. The defendant is a nonresident of the Republic.

February 22, 1845

ADMINISTRATOR'S NOTICE

Shelby County. Estate of Howell Watson (?), deceased. Josiah White, Administrator.

THE RED-LANDER, SAN AUGUSTINE

SUCCESSION

Shelby county. Benjamin E. Waller, late of said county, deceased. E. M. Daggett, Administrator.

March 8, 1845

DIVORCE

Shelby County. George Barber vs. Elisabeth Barber. The defendant is a nonresident of the Republic.

March 15, 1845

SUCCESSION

Shelby County. Estate of Wm. V. Duncan, late of said county, deceased. Apsilla Duncan and Wm. B. Paris, adm'rs.

April 5, 1845

ADMINISTRATION

Jasper County. Estate of Andrew Montgomery, deceased. Wm. S. Keagrey, Administrator.

April 26, 1845

DIVORCE

Houston County. Nancy Warren vs. John Warren. The defendant is a nonresident of the Republic of Texas.

Houston County. Henry E. Wortman vs. Rosanna Wortman. The defendant is a nonresident of the Republic of Texas.

May 15, 1845

DIED

In this city, on the 12th inst., Henry D., son of Mr. Dexter and Mrs. Cornelia Watson, aged fifteen months.

ADMINISTRATOR'S NOTICE

Sabine County. Estate of Willis Murphy, late of the county. Priscilla Murphy, Administratrix.

THE RED-LANDER, SAN AUGUSTINE

June 12, 1845

ADMINISTRATOR'S NOTICE

Houston County. Estate of Phillip Walker, deceased. Martin A. Walker, Adm'r.

Shelby County. Estate of L. U. Edwards, late of said county, deceased. John Edwards, Administrator.

Shelby County. Estate of H. W. K. Myrick, dec'd. John E. Myrick, Adm'r.

September 11, 1845

DIED

In Lexington, Kentucky, on the 28th July, last, Hon. Alexander M. Davis, late Chief Justice of this county. Died at Mrs. Layton's and was buried in the Episcopal burying ground in Lexington.

October 2, 1845

DIED

In this county, on Sunday last, Mrs. Margart F. Thompson, wife of Henry S. Thompson, aged 39 years.

October 16, 1845

MARRIED

On the 5th inst., by Hon. Alfred Polk, Mr. Lucien Lockhart of Washington County, to Miss Novaline Corzine, of this county.

In Nacogdoches County on Thursday evening, Oct. 9, by Hon. W. W. Wingfield, A. A. Nelson to Miss J. C. Simpson.

On Sunday the 5th instant, in the same county, Capt. Wm. M. Simpson to Mrs. Letitia Buford.

In this city on the 9th inst., Mr. C. B. Powell, to Miss Caroline Hamilton.

ADMINISTRATOR'S SALE

In the town of Shelbyville... The property of Nelson Howell, deceased. Also the property of Samuel Roseter, dec'd. Also the property of Harriet Nail, dec'd. Also the property of Ephraim Story, dec'd., all lying in Harrison county on the waters of Murvall's Bayou. Richard Hooper, Adm'r.

THE RED-LANDER, SAN AUGUSTINE

SUCCESSION

Letters of administration upon the estate of Alfred A. George [with the will annexed] were granted to the undersigned, by the Honorable Probate court of Shelby county.
Charles Turner,
Martha A. George, Administrators.

NOTICE

The Chief Justice of Sabine county, Texas.. committed to us the estate of Thomas Yates.
William C. Duffield,
Alexander Horton,
Matthew Cartwright.
Trust's

October 23, 1845

MARRIED

In Washington, on the 26th August, Dr. John S. Ford to Mrs. L. Lewis.

On the 10th inst., by James M. Burroughs, Esq., Mr. William Kirkham to Miss Nancy Slaughter, both of Louisiana.

DIED

At the residence of his father, in Sabine county, on the 7th of October, Mr. Henry Hankly, aged 16 years, three months and 22 days.

October 30, 1845

DIED

A dreadful rencontre happened in Sabine county on Friday last , in which Col. A. B. Means, of Georgia, was shot, and died immediately... He resided for some time in the county of Harrison.

November 6, 1845

ANGELINA STOPPING HOUSE

The subscriber has opened a House of Entertainment on the bank of the Angelina River for the accommodation of travellers at Joseph Durst's Crossing. His house and stables shall be well supplied.   A. C. Denson.

THE RED-LANDER, SAN AUGUSTINE

ADMINISTRATRIX' SALE

Pursuant to an order of the Hon. Probate Court for the county of Shelby, I will offer at public sale... at the residence of Thomas Noble, deceased, all the personal property belonging to the succession of said Thomas Noble.
Susan Noble, Administratrix.

November 13, 1845

MARRIED

This morning (10th September), by the Rev. Mr. Sprole, Col. William Hogan, of Henderson, Rusk county, Texas, to Miss Cornelia Virginia, daughter of James B. Holmes, Esq., of this city.

December 4, 1845

MARRIED

In this county on Thursday last, Mr. Milton Irish to Miss Emily Eves.

On the 19th ult., by A. B. Patton, Esq., Mr. P. J. Hamsley to Miss Eliza Wilson, of this city.

CAUTION

This is to forewarn all persons from digging my land about the Old Mission, as I will enforce the law against any person so offending.
Jas Perkins.

December 11, 1845

EXECUTION

Joseph Simmons was executed on the 28th instant in the town of Shelbyville, for the murder of James Tutt.

January 8, 1846

ADMINISTRATOR'S SALE

By an order of the probate Court of Shelby county, I will sell... the property of John M. Bradley, dec'd.... at the Court house door, in the town of Shelbyville. Richard Hooper, Adm'r.

THE RED-LANDER, SAN AUGUSTINE

January 15, 1846

NOTICE

A letter addressed by the woman of whom we spoke in our last number, to her daughter, Mrs. Elizabeth Clemons, Trenton, Gibson Co., Tennessee... She signs her name Frances Lock... She is now at Mrs. Harris's in Shelby county.

ADMINISTRATOR'S SALE

By order of the Honorable Probate Court of Shelby Co., we will offer for sale... the estate of William V. Duncan, deceased.   W. D. Paris, Administrator,
Apsilla Duncan, Administratrix
of said estate.

February 5, 1846

MARRIED

On the 20th ult., by the Hon. A. Polk, F. B. Dixon, Esq., to Miss Lavinia Shanks, all of this place.

On the 8th ult., by the Rev. H. B. Kelsy, Col. L. H. Mabbitt to Miss Eliza Isabella Taliaferro, all of Marshall, Harrison county.

DIED

At his residence in Sabine county, after a painful illness of twenty one days, on Thursday morning, 29th day of January, 1846, Rev. Littleton Fowler, Presiding Elder of the M. E. Church South, aged 44 years.

February 12, 1846

DIED

On the 5th instant a difficulty occurred between two of our citizens... John F. Jordan and D. C. Miller, that resulted in Miller's being wounded with a knife in the left side of the chest, which caused his death on yesterday morning about 8 o'clock.

ADMINISTRATRIX NOTICE

Letters of administration granted by probate court for Sabine county, on the 18th day of September, 1845, upon the estate of John C. Haile, deceased, notice is hereby given.
Beersheba Davis, Administratrix.

COUNTY OF SABINE

Nancy Ann Childs vs. Abram Childs - Divorce. Said Abram Childs is a non resident of the Republic of Texas.

February 26, 1846

NOTICE

If Wyatt Woodruff Adams, who emigrated to this country some time in 1837, will address a letter to Mr. Swain Williams, Oleander, Marshall county, Alabama, he will hear something greatly to his advantage.

COUNTY OF JASPER

Alfred I. Shelby vs. Robert A. Pennall - Attachment... Founded on a claim against said defendant for the sum of four hundred and fifty three dollars and interest.. The defendent is a non resident of this republic.

March 12, 1846

NOTICE

The undersigned, son and one of the heirs of Edmond Quirk, senior, late of Texas, makes known to all whom it may concern, that he protests against any sale of the real estate of Edmond Quirk senior, deceased, by any and every person under whatsoever pretext; and that he will at a convenient time proceed to claim his interests as one of the heirs of said estate.

Thomas Quirk
Of the Parish of St. Landry, Louisiana.

EX MATRIMONAL NOTICE

Whereas, my wife, Elizabeth Baker, has absconded from my bed and board, without any just cause or provocation, I hereby forwarn all persons from crediting her on my account, as I am determined not to pay any debts of her contracting.

T. Baker.

ESTATE NOTICES

County of Jasper. Zimri Wms. Eddy, administrator of the estate of Stephen H. Everitt, deceased, vs. Thomas C. Bunker, Thomas H. Brenan, David McMahon...

County of Shelby. James Bowlin vs. The Heirs of Jeremiah Bowlin, deceased. Partition. This day appeared

THE RED-LANDER, SAN AUGUSTINE

James Bowlin, and presented his petition praying for a writ of partition of the estate of Jeremiah Bowlin, dec'd., and it appearing to the satisfaction of the court that William Bowlin, Sarah Stanfield, wife of William Stanfield, Polly Waldrop, wife of Claborn Waldrop, and Elizabeth Cornwall, wife of William Cornwall, are now residents of the Republic of Texas.- Therefore it is ordered...

County of Jasper. The undersigned having been appointed administratrix of the estate of Daniel Joslin, deceased, late of Jasper county, at the September term of the Hon. probate court for said county, all persons having claims against said estate are hereby notified to present them.
Martha C. Joslin, Adm'x.

April 2, 1846

NOTICE

Squire M. Baird & W. C. Allison have associated themselves in the practice of Law. Their office is up stairs in the Stone House, where one or both of them will at times be found. Nacogdoches.

April 9, 1846

MARRIED

In Sabine Town on Thursday, April 3rd inst., by the Rev. P. W. Wartener, The Rev. Isaac M. Williams, of the Western Texas Conference, M. E. South, to Miss ... Austin of Sabine Town.

July 15, 1854

OBITUARY

Died on the 17th ult., at the residence of Mrs. Mary DeCamp, in this place, Mrs. Abby DeCamp, aged about 72 years. Abby Donington was born in the state of New Jersey. Her parents emigrated to the city of New York while she was yet small, where she was afterwards married to Mr. Stephen DeCamp and where she remained until after the death of her husband. In 1847, she removed with her son, J. C. DeCamp, to the city of New Orleans, where she remained until after the death of her son, when she accompanied her daughter-in-law to this place, and remained with her until her death.
Mrs. DeCamp was an amiable and pious Christian. In 1809, she united with the Dutch Reformed Church, and remained a consistent member until her death.
Mrs. DeCamp was eminently useful as a Christian. She was a constant attendant upon the ministry of the word; took an active part in promoting the Missionary and Bible cause,

Sabbath Schools, &c, &c, and was constantly engaged in some act of useful benevolence.

After her removal to Texas, finding no church of her own denomination, she became a Parishioner (but not a member), of the Episcopal Church.

She was buried with the rites of the Episcopal Church, Rev. E. H. Downing officiating, and a large number of citizens being present. [N. O. Picayune and New York and Cincinnatti papers please copy.]

July 22, 1854

OBITUARY

Died, at the residence of Mr. Drury Chummey [?] in this county ... July 20th ... Mr. James Randolph Hale, aged 22 years and four months.

DIED

It is our painful duty to anounce the death of our fellow citizen, the Hon. William C. Henry, at his residence in this place...on Thursday night inst...Born in Nashville, Tennessee, on the 5th day of October, a.d. 1817...He leaves a wife and six children.

July, 29, 1854

MARRIED

On the 23rd inst., at Shelbyville, Shelby County, Texas, by Hiram Cozart, Esq., Mr. John Davenport to Miss Nellie Hagan both of Reynolds Circus. [Reynolds and Look's New York Circus was touring in East Texas.] (P.S. New Orleans Delta and Austin papers, please copy.)

COUNTY OF SHELBY

Whereas, on the 29th day of January 1853, Robert McWilliams filed his petition,... complains of Martha Buford and Thomas J. Buford defendants, in this, that the said Martha Buford by the name and description of Martha Foster on the 13th day of August, 1850, signed and delivered to Hiram Allen her writing obligatory. Defendant Thomas J. Buford's residence is unknown to plaintiff.

COUNTY OF SHELBY

D. Brittain. & Co. vs. Z. C. Johnson. Said defendant is absent from the State. To answer D. Brittain & R. R. Wiggins, merchants and partners.

THE RED-LANDER, SAN AUGUSTINE

August 12, 1854

HOMICIDE

We sincerely regret to state that a man by the name of W. H. Lowry was killed on Monday last, in this place, by Thomas Willingham. Lowry had taken a walk in company with a man by the name of Dupree in the outskirts of town, and on his return was waylaid and shot with a double barrelled shot-gun, he fell mortally wounded, was taken to the office of Dr. Roberts where he expired after four hours of the most intense suffering.

OBITUARY

Died, in San Augustine, Texas, August 6th, 1854, after a protracted illness, Mrs. Harriet Caroline Berry, consort of Gen. John G. Berry. The subject of this notice was the daughter of Barnes and Rachel Clark, she was born 22d Dec. 1808, and married to John G. Berry 2d Dec. 1824, in Lincoln county, Tennessee, joined the Baptist Church at Bethel in said county in the year 1828, and remained an exemplary and consistent member, until her removal to San Augustine in the year 1837.

September 9, 1854

DIED

In Shelbyville, Shelby County, on Wednesday the 30th of August, of measles, Mr. Malcolm Sinclair, aged about 38 years.

September 16, 1854

MARRIED

On Thursday, the 31st of August, our old and much beloved friend, Van Walling to Miss Mary Ann Thomas, all of Shelby county.

DIED

In this place on Wednesday the 6th inst., of Billious fever, Mr. Jno. Pryor Campbell, of Pike county, Georgia, in the 26th year of his age.

September 23, 1854

MARRIED

In this county on Thursday evening the 15th inst., at

the residence of her father Edward Willingham, Esq., by the Rev. J. Crawford, Miss Sarah F. Willingham to Mr. Willis M. Murphy of Sabine county.

                            MURDER

    Mr. Medford by John Erwin. [Cherokee Sent.]

                           OBITUARY

    Horatio M. Hanks, died on the 1st inst. of [bilious fever ?]. Left a widow, the former Nancy Thacker, and several young children. Parents were Peter [?] and Isabella [?] H. Hanks. [long obituary but difficult to read.]

                       December 9, 1854

                            DIED

    In Nacogdoches, on the 2d inst., Mr. Lacey G. Hubert, in the 23d year of his age.

    In Nacogdoches, on the 3d inst., Col. Frost Thorn, in the 61st year of his age.

                      ADMINISTRATOR'S SALE

    Shelby County. Selling property of Wm. Todd, deceased. E. B. Dysart, Administrator.

NACOGDOCHES TIMES

April 29, 1848

ATTENTION

There will be a muster of Company A, in the town of Nacogdoches, on the first Monday in May, for the purpose of a drill. The members of the company are requested to attend in accordance to law. April 8, 1848. By order of JAS. HART, Capt. Com. Comp. A.

PROSPECTUS OF THE NACOGDOCHES TIMES

The first number of the Nacogdoches Times was issued on the 31st July, and is designed to be a permanent journal. The encouragement which this paper has already received, without effort to obtain subcribers, is gratifing to its conductors, and encourages them to believe that its circulation and utility may be increased by the issuance of a prospectus.

The Times will be devoted to the promotion and advancement of all the important interests of our State, and every means available will be used to render it interesting and useful to its patrons. Solid and useful literature, knowledge of those branches of the sciences of daily practice and utility, and especially science connected with agriculture, may be generallly and to good purpose, diffused through the medium of a newspaper. To these much attention will be paid, and we hope to render the TIMES of the highest importance to the farmer, by collecting and disseminating useful information on the subject of Agriculture.

In regard to politics, our course shall be that of strict and impartial neutrality. Public men and public measures may be fully discussed through our columns, regard being had to that decorum and propriety without which a public journal sinks into a vehicle of slander and abuse.

The necessity of a newspaper in the town of Nacogdoches has long been felt, and still exists. A large number of counties will always feel a natural affiliation to the county of Nacogdoches, having for so long a time been united together. There is but one paper published in this large region of country, possessing the highest advantages, and rapidly settling with a population equalling any in our State, and whose interests should not suffer for some means of bringing into public notice the advantages which this part of Texas offers to emigrants settling in our favored State.

Terms - Three Dollars if paid in advance. Four Dollars within six months. Five Dollars at the end of the year. Subscriptions paid in two months will be considered in advance.

FLOYD H. KENDALL, PUBLISHER
NACOGDOCHES TIMES

NACOGDOCHES TIMES

June 3, 1848

THE NEW CATHOLIC CHURCH

As if by magic, a modest and symmetrical little church, dressed in white and green, with its neat cupola and pillars without, organ gallery and other suitable fittings within, has in the last few months raised its head in our little village, through the enterprising zeal of two French gentleman of the clerical profession, from France. This church, we learn, will be consecrated the 11 instant, services be commenced at 9 o'clock A.M., and a Catholic clergyman from Galveston be in attendance.

June 10, 1848

SAN AUGUSTINE

We see from the San Augustine Union that the citizens of that place and vicinity are making the necessary preparations for the celebration of the 4th of July. We wonder if time honored Old Nacogdoches does not intend celebrating it also. If she does, it is time she should be making some preparation. We would suggest the propriety of having a meeting as soon as practicable, to make the necessary arrangements - say Saturday the 17th inst. at 5 o'clock p.m. in the Court-house.

HIGHWAYS AND BY-WAYS

As this the 10th inst. is fixed upon for the general labor of the town people upon the highways, it is suggested that if not out of order, a certain by-way should be amended, viz: the short street west of the University, which is very much worn and washed by rains from long neglect, and when wet and slippery, is difficult for the young ladies (who take that course to and from school) to pass.

RELIGIOUS NOTICE

The Rev. Mr. Sansom, of the Protestant Episcopal Church, will hold divine service in the Court-house, tomorrow evening, 11th inst., at early candle light. Rev. R. Hennesy having arrived, the Catholic Church will be consecrated tomorrow, as announced in our last.

July 8, 1848

RELIGIOUS NOTICE

The Rev. Mr. Sansom will discourse on the subject of Christianity, in the Courthouse, at early candle-lighting

NACOGDOCHES TIMES

Friday evening next, the 14th inst., when he will organize the Protestant Episcopal church. On the following Lord's day, he will preach at 10 o'clock A.M. and at early candle-lighting.

August 5, 1848

OBITUARY

"In the midst of life, we are in death."
Departed this life, on Saturday last, ... o'clock p.m., after a short illness of ... days, Mrs. Matilda Johns, consort of David Johns, Douglass. She died in hope of a glorious immortality.

September 2, 1848

MARRIED

In Douglass, Texas, on the evening of the 24th inst., by the Rev. J. M. Becton, Mr. Andrew J. Sparks, to Miss Mary Ann, daughter of Dr. Elijah Allen, all of this county.

October 12, 1848

MARRIED

On Tuesday evening the 26th ult., by the Rev. John C. Woolam, the Rev. Silas W. Camp, to Miss Martha M. Haltom, all of Rusk county, Texas.

November 25, 1848

DISTRICT COURT

The District Court of our county, owing to the absence of Judge Roberts, who was detained by the inclemency of the weather, did not commence its session until Tuesday afternoon of last week. The Courthouse, although greatly improved, being without a chimney or stove, there was but little business done in the way of trials; and after an ineffectual attempt to obtain a stove, the Court took refuge in the lower story of Mr. Orton's brick house under our office.
We trust that prompt measures will be taken, to render the Court house comfortable and usable. Business cannot be easily transacted with the bench, bar, jury and spectators huddled together in a small room, devoid of seats and proper accommodations; and had it not been for the accidental vacancy of the room used, the Court would have probably been obliged to adjourn for milder weather-- at this season of the year rather an indefinite time.

December 9, 1848

DISTRICT COURT

Our District Court adjourned over from Saturday, December 2nd, to next Monday one week. The adjournment was urged upon the Court by the whole bar, and pretty much all the jurymen and witnesses. The fact was, all were worried out by the cold rain and unpleasant weather, the absence of any preparation for warming the Court house, and the impossibility of getting witnesses to attend in such stormy seasons. "His Honor" therefore adjourned for a week, no doubt hoping that the weather would finish its "blow out" and behave decently. This week, we regret to say, it has acted for some time in a "most violent and outrageous manner: first it blew, then it snew, then it thaad, and then it friz horrid." We have had cold water enough for an army of Sons of Temperance, and some "dreadful examples" have been heard to say that, "The water would get in;" a remarkable fact, not before known to our oldest inhabitant. We learn that the Angelina river is on top its banks, and that there is no doubt the steamboat will leave Pattonia, with a full freight of cotton for the Pass.

April 28, 1849

MARRIED

Married by the Rev. R. B. Wells, on Thursday the 19th instant, in Nacogdoches County, Mr. A. B. Woodward to Miss Nancy E. Whitaker, daughter of B. F. Whitaker, Esq., all of Nacogdoches County.

June 23, 1849

OBITUARY

Died, at the town of Santa Rosa, Mexico, on 2d May, 1848, of Asiatic colera, DEWITT C. CLARK, in the 26th year of his age, son of Amos Clark Esq., of this place.

We little thought, when a few months since, we mentioned the departure of Mr. Clark for California, with his friends Messrs. Hammond and Kendall, that we should so soon chronicle his death.

Full of hopes, and in firm health, Mr. Clark left his home in pursuit of wealth and reputation, taking with him the best wishes of those who had known him from his earlier years. Of manners affable, and a temper kind and generous, he won regard even from those who differed with him; and we are not aware that in this place he left a resentment to bury in his grave. But he has gone, in the morning of life, and in the order of an inscrutable providence, that road all must once pass.

Although when his eyes opened for the last time upon earth and sky, they fell not upon the scenery of his home;

NACOGDOCHES TIMES

although the sod which covers him freshens with the dews of a strange clime; and although he drew his closing breath among a foreign people, and amid strange tongues; yet the last earthly sounds that fell on the ear of the dying man, were home tones of sympathy, affection and support, responsive to his sad remembrance of his parents, and his sister; and that same kindness watched by the coffin till it was lost in the tomb. Be it ever to the honor of Mr. Hammond, that with Mr. Kendall stricken down, and with his comrade dead, he stayed when others fled; and that, if friendship and nursing, triumphing over the dread of pestilence, and the weariness of watching, could have saved life, his friend would have lived.

To the family and friends of the deceased we proffer-alas, how little can such regrets avail to temper sorrow - our sincere sympathy and condolence, in the blow thus suddenly dealt to their hopes and expectations.

August 4, 1849

NOTICE

Mr. Hobart is still at the Planter's hotel, taking Daguerreotypes in a style superior to any that have been taken heretofore in this place. He will remain a week longer, affording opportunity to those of the vicinity who wish correct likenesses, to obtain them.

NACOGDOCHES CHRONICLE

September 4, 1852

MARRIED

On Friday, the 27th ult., by the Rev. J. C. Woolam, Mr. J. P. P. Wilkins to Miss M. A. Hughes, all of this county.

DIED

At the residence of Frost Thorn, Esq., of this city, on the 31st ultimo after a protracted illness, Madam O. V. Bonamy, about 37 years of age.- During her severe illness she showed great fortitude and received the devoted attention of her friends.
She was a lady of high intellectual attainments, firm of character, respected and esteemed by all her acquaintances and beloved by those with whom she was intimately acquainted.

September 18, 1852

DIED

In this place, on the 16th inst., Lavina, daughter of W. M. and Sarah Ann Moore, aged about five years. The words of our Savior are, "Suffer little children to come unto me, for of such is the kingdom of Heaven."

Hon. Bennett H. Martin, presiding judge of the Ninth Judicial District (Texas).

September 25, 1852

DIED

At the residence of her father, --- Whitaker, Esq., near Douglas, a few days since, Miss America Whitaker, aged 12 years.

October 9, 1852

NOTICE

We hope our hotel-keepers and merchants will bear in mind that the Grand Lodge of Texas [Masonic] meets in this place in January next, and that it will be necessary to have plenty to eat, and good, comfortable rooms, with fire-places, or stoves in them, enough to accommodate three or four hundred persons. Every intelligent citizen of the place would, of course, feel mortified and crest-fallen should a number of persons visit our town and be unable to get comfortable quarters: yet such will inevitably be the case, unless some preparations are made for their reception. It is to be hoped that our hotel- keepers will see that all the vacant rooms about town that have fire-places are fitted up for the occasion. We are well aware of one thing, that Nacogdoches can do such things up "brown," and we hope she will outdo herself, even, in this instance.

DIED

Colonel James Powers, an old Texian, of '26, died lately in Refugio county. Col. P. was formerly a member of the Texas Congress.

October 16, 1852

NOTICE

LINN FLAT.- Our readers will bear in mind that the sale of lots in this new town will take place on Friday and Saturday, the 5th and 6th of November.

MAIL

The mail is now carried in handsome two-horse coaches three times a week between this place and Henderson.

DIED

Mrs. Mary Ann Lott, consort of the Hon. E. E. Lott, died in Tyler on the seventh instant, aged thirty years.

October 23, 1852

MARRIED

In San Augustine, on the 11th instant by the Rev. E. Downing, James Holman, Esq., of Grand Ecore, La., to Miss Mary J. Thomas.

On the 3d instant, by the Rev. Edward Fontaine, Washington L. Hill, to Mrs. Mary A. Hervey, both of Austin.

Another.- It becomes our pleasing duty to Chronicle the escape from all the evils of bachelordom, of our friend, W. M. Messenger, of the Flag of the Union. We have mislaid the paper containing the announcement, and do not recollect the lady's name, but one thing is certain- Messenger is married!

October 30, 1852

OBITUARY

Died, at the residence of Dr. John L. Windham, on the 16th instant, at 4 o'clock p.m., Mr. James B. McDaniel aged 21 years. Mr. McDaniel was a native of Butts county, Ga.- a young man of promise. Last winter he left his parents, relatives and friends, to seek his fortune in this, our western clime: he succeeded in business until taken with chills and fever, which was partially cured, but having taken cold, settled upon his lungs, and caused his death.
T'is true our friend had no affectionate mother, sister or relation near to sooth him in his dying moments -
To make his dying couch lie
Smooth "as downy pillows are."
although he had friends who watched with anxious eyes the last struggling of the departed spirit until it took its exit from this to a fairer and brighter clime.

To his berieved [sic] parents we remark he died calm and composed; all that seemed to trouble him in his dying moments, as he was deprived of the society of his parents. The last words that fell from the lips of the deceased was, "Oh, that I were back in my own, my native Georgia and if deprived of that privilege, may I meet my mother and father, brother and sisters, in that haven of rest where
parting will be no more."   Chireno, Texas, J. G. C.

OUR STREETS

We notice, with much pleasure, the efforts that are being made by the "city fathers" towards improving our streets. The bridge across the La Nana, and street near it, have been placed in excellent condition, and other streets greatly improved. The work has been done by Mr. George Clevinger, under the supervision of the mayor and aldermen.

November 16, 1852

OBITUARY

Death of W. M. Moore

To the W. P., Officers and Brothers of Nacogdoches Division, No. 3,   Sons of Temperance.

Your Committee on Resolutions respectfully report. That whereas the Great Patriarch of the Universe having in His wise Providence visited our circle of brotherhood with affliction and deprived it of a highly esteemed member, We, therefore, as a token of our deep regret for this afflictive dispensation of Divine wisdom, do unanimously adopt the following resolutions.-
Resolved, That the hand of Death has fallen heavily upon us, in depriving us of our lamented brother, W. M. Moore,

and we deeply sympathise with the friends and relatives, who, in the person of the deceased, have lost a counsellor and a friend.

Resolved, That we most especially sympathise with the family of the deceased, for the loss of an affectionate and prudent husband, a kind and indulgent father.

Resolved, That, in respect to the memory of our brother, we wear the usual badge of mourning for thirty days.

Resolved, That the foregoing resolutions be published in the Nacogdoches Chronicle, and a copy of them presented to the afflicted family.

Submitted in Love, Purity and Fidelity.

H. C. Hancock
W. H. Lyon
J. C. Harrison

November 23, 1852

EMIGRATION TO EASTERN TEXAS

The following paragaph is cut from the Fort Smith [Ark] Herald of the 30th ult.: We were informed, on Wednesday last, by a gentleman just in from Texas, that he passed on the road hundreds of wagons belonging to emigrants bound for Texas. He passed, in two days, sixty wagons near Middle Boggy. About forty wagons passed through this place on Monday and Tuesday, and still they come. The road is crowded with them. Such an emigration has not been known for several years.

MARRIED

At the residence of Major W. Hollis, on the 16th inst., By Rev. E. H. Downing, Mr. John C. Rohte to Miss Jane Hollis all of San Augustine.

THE FIRST THREE HUNDRED FAMILIES

Of this illustrious band of pioneers and patriots introduced into the province of Texas, by Gen. Stephen F. Austin, only nineteen heads of families are now remaining.

December 7, 1852

DIED

In San Augustine, on the 29th day of November, Greenville H. , Son of G. H. and Sarah T. Patterson, in the 17th year of his age.

NACOGDOCHES CHRONICLE

NOTICE

General Houston will arrive in this place next Thursday evening, on his way to Washington City.

IN THE DARK

Our friend of the Henderson Flag announces in his last paper, that 'Richard S. Walker, Esq., of San Augustine,' is spoken of as a candidate for Congress. Why, friend Estell, we are really afraid you do not 'take the papers.' We are willing to admit that San Augustine is the 'Athens of Texas'; that she has many clever citizens and bridgeless creeks, but we can't give up to her our Dick Walker.

December 14, 1852

OBITUARY

Death of W. H. Cushney, Esq.- Our old and highly valued friend, William H. Cushney, of Austin, is dead. Mr. Cushney was an old Texian, an honest man, and a true patriot. Our acquaintance with him dates back to the days of our boyhood, and while we live the memory of W. H. Cushney will be cherished in at least one grateful heart.

OBITUARY

Colonel John W. Crockett, a son of the celebrated David Crockett, who fell at the Alamo, died in Memphis, Tennessee, a few days ago. Col. Crockett was several years a member of Congress from Tennessee, but for the last few years has been living in New Orleans.

January 4, 1853

OBITUARIES

Death of Charles Chevaillier.- It becomes our painful duty to announce the demise, on the 30th ult., of our old and enterprising citizen, Charles Chevaillier, Esq. Mr. Chevaillier has been one of our leading merchants for many years, and was a thorough going business man. He was a man of most untiring industry; no difficulties, however great, could overcome his energies. He came amongst us, eighteen years ago, a very poor man, but by his unwearied exertions, soon won his way to the front rank of wealthy merchants. He leaves a most interesting family to mourn his loss. May the God of the fatherless and the widow afford them protection and consolation in this hour of sad bereavement! The Episcopal burial service was performed by Rev. E. H. Downing, after which the Masonic fraternity deposited the remains of Mr.

Chevaillier in their last resting place with appropriate honors.

Death of Mrs. Kaufman.- A friend in San Augustine has forwarded to us the mournful intelligence of the death of this estimable lady. Our correspondent thus details the sad event:
"Died, at her residence in Sabine Town, Texas, on Sunday morning, the 19th December, 1852, Mrs. Jane R. Kaufman, widow of the late Hon. David S. Kaufman, Representative in Congress from this District." Mrs. K. was highly esteemed by all who knew her, and her loss will be mourned by a large circle of sincere and devoted friends.

Died, at his residence in this county, on Monday, the 20th day of December, of bilious pneumonia, Thomas Alders, aged about 48 years. The life of Mr. Alders was an illustration of the truth of the poet's saying, "An honest man's the noblest work of God."

MARRIED

Near this place, on the 1st instant by James Hart, Esq., Mr. Henry Voigt to Miss Margaretta Tohlen.

At the same time and place, and by the same, Mr. Ludwig Kunolt to Miss Catherine Kracks.

At the same time and place, and by the same, Mr. Henry Schroeder to Miss Frederika Buschmeyer.

On the 13th inst., by Rev. B. Eaton, Maj. Thos. B. Howard, of Fort Bend county, to Miss Sue L., daughter of Dr. John Price, late of Galveston.

By A. G. Cantley, Esq., on the second inst., at the residence of Elton A. Campbell, Esq., Mr. George W. Campbell to Miss Martha Evans, all of Anderson county.

January 11, 1853

MARRIED

In this county, on the 6th inst., by James Hart, Esq., Mr. Franklin Rector to Miss Sarah Frances Johnson.

In this place, on the 9th inst., by James Hart, Esq., Mr. Pleasant Wright to Mrs. Malinda Gann.

The family of Attorney-General Jennings have arrived in our place, with the intention, we understand, of taking up

their residence here. Col. Jennings formerly resided in
Nacogdoches, and our citizens will be glad to hear of his
return.

DIED

The Cherokee Sentinel announces the death of William
B. Davis, of Rusk. Mr. D. was a young lawyer of much promise.

February 1, 1853

JAMES H. DURST

Mr. Thomas G. Gardner, of San Antonio, informs us
that just before he left home a rumour came in from the Rio
Grande, that Maj. James H. Durst had been assassinated by two
Mexicans in the employ of the Mexican Government. We attach
very little importance to the report, but give it for what it
is worth. Mr. G. says that Clay Davis, Maj. Durst's partner,
was absent on duty as captain of a ranging company, and that
the Mexican Government, out of revenge, for the aid given by
Maj. D. to Carvajal last winter, sent over two Mexicans, and
that they, after stabbing Maj. Durst in the heart, succeeded
in making their escape to the west bank of the Rio Grande
in a canoe.

February 15, 1853

MARRIED

On the 12th inst., at the residence of John J.
Simpson, Esq., near Nacogdoches, by Judge Blake, Mr. Condy
Raguet, to Miss Francis A. Simpson.

At the residence of Dr. G. S. Hyde, near this place
on the 8th inst., by James Hart, Esq., Mr. Henderson
Muckleroy, to Miss Mary C. Kendall, all of this county.

March 29, 1853

DIED

In this place on Wednesday the 16th inst., about 8
o'clock, after an illness of several days, William C. Johnson,
an old and esteemed citizen of Nacogdoches. Mr. Johnson was a
man of much benevolence and kindness of heart. He was buried
with Masonic honors, and an eloquent and appropriate funeral
address delivered by the Rev. Simpson Shepherd.

NACOGDOCHES CHRONICLE

April 12, 1853

MARRIED

At the residence of A. H. Crain, Esq., four miles east of this place, on Thursday last, the 7th instant, by H. Nelson, Esq., Benjamin L. Rusk, Esq., [son of our distinguished townsman, Gen. T. J. Rusk] to Miss Rachael Crain, daughter of Giles Crain, Esq., of Harrison county.

We offer our warmest congratulations to the happy couple, and assure our friend "Ben"- ah! beg pardon, he's a married man now Mr. Rusk - that looks more dignified - that he has our best wishes for the happiness and prosperity of himself and bride. May they find their pathway through life, strewn with flowers, ever blooming and ever fresh.

The wedding of our friend Rusk, was duly honored. The slendid supper at A. H. Crain's where the marriage took place, is said to have been superb. The substantials and luxuries of life were furnished in sufficient profusion to satisfy the veriest gourmands and epicures, that any country could afford. The succeeding evening a brilliant party was given at the residence of Gen. Rusk, at which the beauty, wit, and fashion of Nacogdoches, and vicinity were duly represented, and "All went merry as a marriage ball."

DIED

In this place, on Sunday night, at about 12 p.m. of Typhus Fever, Mr. Solomon Binsgenstorfer, aged sixty-three years. Mr. B. was a native of Switzerland, and was generally esteemed here as an honest, industrious and well-disposed citizen.

April 19, 1853

ESCAPED

A fellow who has been in the jail in this place, for some time past awaiting his trial under a charge of horse-stealing, made his escape on the night of the 15th inst., and having helped himself to a horse belonging to O. L. Holmes, Esq., and a saddle and blanket the property of H. Nelson, Esq., left for parts unknown. We presume efforts are being made for his re-capture.

SUNDAY SCHOOL

The initiatory steps were taken on Sunday last, for the establishment of a Union Sunday school in Nacogdoches. There was quite a respectable turnout of teachers and scholars. The school will be fully organized next Sunday at 9 o'clock, A.M. We trust that our citizens will foster this enterprise. The ladies, particularly are invited to be present. It may be as well to state that the school meets in the Court House, and will be through in time for Church services.

ACQUITTED

Mr. Runnels, son of Ex-Governor Runnels, who was on trial in Montgomery county, for killing Hansborough, has been acquitted. He was ably defended by Messrs. W. P. Rogers, of Washington, Jones Rivers, of Columbus, and Peter W. Gray, of Houston.

April 26, 1853

DIED

In Nacogdoches, on Thursday last of Typhoid Pneumonia, Horatio Nelson, Esq., an old and esteemed citizen. Mr. Nelson was a native of Maine, but emigrated to Texas at an early day, and has ever proved himself a good citizen and that "noblest work of God, an honest man." His remains were attended to the grave, by Rankin Lodge, No. 18, I.O.O.F., and Nacogdoches Division, No. 3, Sons of Temperance, of both of which orders he was a prominent member.

May 3, 1853

DIED

Among the passengers who started from New Orleans for Galveston on the Louisiana, was the aged father of our fellow-citizen, A. S. Ruthven, Esq. Sad to relate, when the steamer was within a few hours sail of Galveston, the aged man, worn down by the fatigue of a long journey from Edinburgh, Scotland, expired. His affectionate son and his lady were anxiously awaiting his arrival. Their grief may be better imagined than described when the steamer arrived with the mournful intelligence of his death.
- Houston Paper.

MARRIED

On the 28th ult., at the residence of Hon. Amos Clark, by Chief Justice Blake, Thos. A. Nickerson, Esq., member of the Bar at Shelby, to Miss Martha A. Scott, of this city.

May 10, 1853

MYSTERIOUS DISAPPEARANCE

It becomes our duty as public journalists, to record

a most singular circumstance that has lately transpired in our town. On last Saturday, about 2 o'clock in the morning, four of the cleverest young gentlemen we have, disappeared just as the stage was leaving for San Augustine and have not been heard of since. Whether their object is to commit suicide or matrimony, we are unable to say.

P.S. Since writing the above, the young gentlemen have returned, minus a hat and several hearts. We learn from them that the object of their visit, was to present a couple of bell[e]s to two of the churches at San Augustine. Such benevolence is worthy of commendation.

May 17, 1853

DIED

We regret to announce the death of Mrs. Kozia C. Blake, consort of the Hon. Bennett Blake, Chief Justice of this county. This estimable lady, departed this life, after an illness of several months, on Sunday, the 15th inst. Her remains were followed to the grave by a large concourse of our citizens.

SUICIDE

An individual - stranger - whose name has since been ascertained to be J. F. Arnot, of Texas, walked into the Court House on Monday evening, and deliberately blew out his brains with a pistol charge. The report was heard and the body was soon discovered. It was a ghastly object, weltering in the blood which formed a pool beneath the body. Montgomery, Ala. Journal.

May 31, 1853

VISITOR

BEN McCULLOUGH.- This celebrated Texas Ranger, now U.S. Marshall for Texas, spent a few days in our town last week. He looks as though he was able to do his country much service yet. The Major was the guest of Gen. Rusk, during his stay with us.

A NEW COACH

We notice that Col. A. Houston has put a new coach on his line between this place and Huntsville, that is of Texas manufacture, we believe, altogether. The work was done at Huntsville, and does credit alike to the enterprise of Col. Houston, and the skill of the workman who constructed it. We had the pleasure of a ride in the new coach on Friday last for which we were indebted to the politeness of Mr. Sharp.

VISITOR

We had the pleasure of a visit from Gen. James H. Rogers, of Cass county, during the past week. The General has recovered from a severe spell of sickness, but is rapidly regaining his accustomed good looks.

DEATH OF THE HON. BERNARD E. BEE

We regret to learn, through a private letter to Maj. Simpson of our city, that the Hon. Bernard E. Bee, formerly Secretary of War of our Republic, died very recently at his residence in Pendleton, South Carolina.- Col. Bee during his life, has sustained the high reputation for strict integrity and honor, for superior talents and for the most exemplary deportment in all the private relations of life. During his residence in Texas Col. Bee discharged the laborious and responsible duties of secretary of War in a manner that gave, we believe, universal satisfaction. And when on account of ill health, he finally returned to his native State, we do not believe he left an enemy behind him, although the country was unfortunately destracted with personal and party animosities among most of our leading men. The memory of Col. Bee will be cherished as one among the earliest advocates of our independence, and as one of the most high minded and honorable patriots who ever embarked in the cause of human liberty.
--Gal. News.

June 14, 1853

GEN. SAM HOUSTON

Will address the people of Nacogdoches, at the Court-House, this afternoon, at two o'clock. The "Old Hero" is in fine health and spirits, and our citizens may expect to be entertained in his usual happy manner.

The Rt. Rev. Bishop Freeman, of the Protestant Episcopal Church, has been preaching in our town for a week past. He has been assisted in his labors by Rev. E. H. Downing.

June 21, 1853

COL. M. T. JOHNSON'S RESIDENCE

Col. DeMorse, editor of the Standard, who has lately been traveling through the upper Trinity country, thus describes the residence of Col. Johnson - a place noted for its historic interest as connected with the trying times of the Lone Star Republic:

Immediately before the house, is a large double oak, under which the treaty of 1842, with the assembled tribes of Indians, was made by Gen'ls Tarrant and Terrell and John Durst as Commissioners, under the immediate supervision of President Houston, who was present. From a projecting limb waved the flag of the Lone Star, and the historical incident will probably perpetuate the tree. It has been mostly shorn of its limbs this spring, with a view to reinvigorate it. The Colonel is noted for hospitality, and everybody who comes is expected to feel at home, and make himself as much at home as possible with the ample room and comforts of the establishment.

DEATHS

In this place on Thursday last, of Dropsy of the heart, Thomas C. Barret, an old and esteemed citizen of Nacogdoches. Mr. Barret was born in Virginia in 1821, and was, at the time of death, in his 33d year. In 1832, his parents emigrated to Tennessee, and in 1837, to Texas: since which time he has resided in this county. He has left a widow, three small children, and a large circle of relatives and friends to mourn his loss. May that Being who protects the fatherless and the widow, afford them strong consolation in this hour of trial. [Also a tribute to Barret by Milam Lodge Masons on same date and page.]

Died. - In this place, on Sunday last, of Consumption, Dr. George H. Livingston.

July 12, 1853

TO NEWSPAPER PUBLISHERS

William Jasper, a youth, aged about 14 or 15, ran away from this office without excuse or provocation, on last Friday night. It is supposed he went to his father's, in Cherokee county; and will probably attempt to get work in some other printing office. We warn publishers not to employ him. We had contracted with his father for his services for five years, but after staying some 15 months, until he gained a fair knowledge of typesetting, so that he could be a little useful, and make some return for the time and trouble spent in giving him the information, - he left us in the night and without our knowledge. We trust that no publisher would have so little regard for the rights and interests of newspaper publishers as to encourage him in this desertion.
July 9th,' 1853.   MOORE & HARRISON

August 2, 1853

MARRIED

At the residence of Geo. B. Perry, Esq., in Nacogdoches county, on the 13th July, by the Rev. Neill Brown, Mr. William A. Pope, of Rusk, Cherokee county, to Miss Octavio E. Perry, of Nacogdoches county, Texas, being attended by a large number of respectable guests, at their respective feastive boards.
> Together may they sweetly live,
> Together may they die,
> And each a stately crown receive,
> And reign above the sky.

August 29, 1853

KILLING

A gentleman, recently from the upper Brazos, informs us, that at Moseley's Landing, in Burleson county, a man by the name of Brazle was killed, a few days since, by a Mr. Smith. It seems that the deputy Sheriff, was endeavoring to arrest a Dr. Lucky who was secreted at the house of Brazle. Brazle endeavored to shoot the officer, when Mr. Smith, who had been summoned to assist in the arrest, fired upon, and killed him.

September 6, 1853

VISITOR

Ex-Governor Henderson, spent several days in Nacogdoches during the last week.

EXPEDITION

J. C. Harrison, Esq., the editor of this paper, accompanied Gen. Rusk on the expedition to El Paso. He has been suffering from ill-health some months, and goes to snuff the fresh breeze of the prairies as a remedy. We hope to see him back, renewed in mental and physical energy in a few months.

September 20, 1853

DIED

At the residence of her husband, near this place on the 14th inst., Mrs. Rebecca White, wife of James D. White, aged 30 years.

September 27, 1853

HANGING

Fitzgerald, who murdered Robinson at Saledo, last Spring, has been taken from the officers at that place, and hung. The citizens of that place must have but little confidence in the ability of the law to deal full justice.

DIED

Of the prevailing epidemic, on Friday, the 12th August, Capt. Benjamin F. Hunt, father-in-law of Col. Buckner H. Payne.

On Monday the 5th inst., Mary Hunt, infant daughter of Mary J. and Buckner H. Payne. [from the N.O. Pic.]

This sad news will be received with regret by the many friends of these two families in this vicinity. Capt. Hunt was formerly a resident of Nacogdoches.

RESOLUTION OF DOUGLASS LODGE

Douglass Lodge Room.
Sept. 17th, A.D. 1853, A.L. 5853.

Whereas, this Lodge has learned with deep regret of the death of our worthy Brother, John M. Becton, a minister of the Presbyterian church.
Resolved, As members of this Lodge, we deeply deplore and lament our much esteemed Brother.
Resolved, That we most sincerely sympathize with the family of our beloved Brother, and devoutly commend them to the kind care of him who has promised to be the Father of the fatherless and a husband to the widow.
Resolved, That as a mark of our esteem for our deceased Brother we will wear the usual badge of mourning for the space of thirty days.
Resolved, That the Secretary be requested to send a copy of these resolutions to the bereaved family of the deceased and to the Nacogdoches Chronicle, and Masonic Signet, with the request that they publish the same.

L. B. WARD,
O. H. BOYKIN,
S. H. BOREN,
Committee

October 18, 1853

OBITUARY

At a special meeting of Kaufman Lodge, No. 115, the

following resolutions were unanimously adopted:

Whereas it has pleased Almighty God, in the dispensation of his providence, to remove by death our worthy and beloved brother, Alfred G. Sims, who died at his residence in Rusk county, on the 24th of August, 1853,

Resolved, That in the death of our Brother, this Lodge has lost one of its most zealous and devoted members – the community a valuable citizen and his family a kind husband and an affectionate parent.

Resolved, That we deeply mourn the death of our Brother, and cordially sympathize with his bereaved widow and orphans, and friends, in this their deep affliction.

Resolved, That as a token of our love and esteem for our deceased brother, the members of this Lodge wear the usual badge of mourning for thirty days.

Resolved, That a copy of these poceedings be forwarded to the editor of the Nacogdoches Chronicle, with a request to publish; also a copy to the family and friends of the deceased.

E. W. Bailey, Sec'y pro tem.

OBITUARY

Whereas it has pleased an Allwise Creator and Governor of the Universe to take from the stage of action and usefulness among us, our much beloved and highly esteemed companion Simon Z. Sanford, of Mount Vernon Chapter, No. 25, who died in Freestone county, Texas, on the 15th day of July, in the 26th year of his age; Therefore –

Resolved, 1, That as a token of our respect for his memory, and the bright example he set among us while living, the Companions of Mount Vernon Chapter will wear the usual badges of mourning for thirty days.

Resolved, 2, That a copy of these proceedings be sent to Pine Bluff Lodge, No. 85, as a token of esteem and thankfulness to those Brothers for their untiring attention to our deceased Brother, during his last illness and burial.

Resolved, 3, That, as an evidence of our esteem of his good qualities and many virtues, and of our sympathy with them in their great loss, a copy of these resolutions and preamble be sent to his parents.

Resolved, 4, That the Nacogdoches Chronicle and the Masonic Signet each be requested to publish.

E. M. DAGGETT, Ch'n;
J. L. BRIDGES,
A. E. HANDLEY.

MARRIED

Near this place, on the 16th inst., by James Hart, J. P., Mr. Wm. G. Deen, to Mrs. Sarah Brantley, all of this county.

NACOGDOCHES CHRONICLE

October 25, 1853

MARRIED

On the 24th inst., by James Hart, Esq., Mr. Clemente Mansola, to Miss Theodora Acosta, all of this county.

November 8, 1853

STEAM SHIP

Two of our most social and enterprising citizens left us during the past week in the persons of Messrs. Bondies and Rohte, the former the captain and latter the Clerk of the steamer Kate. They go to take command of her and will commence business immediately on their arrival. She will make regular trips from Magnolia on the Trinity to Galveston. As a good-humored, whole-souled gentleman, the Captain is beyond our commendation. As for Mr. Rohte, we can say on the score of personal acquaintance and attachment that his warm heart and generous qualities will continue to make him a favorite on the river. No "Kate" could be in better hands.

DEATH

The funeral sermon of Thos. C. Barret, dec'd, was preached in this place on Sunday last, by Rev. A. S. Hayter. A large congregation of the friends of the deceased attended from the town and country. The Reverend gentleman was laboring under a severe indispositon at the time, and we regret to learn was quite ill after the sermon. His proceeding at all, under such circumstances, has won him the grateful thanks of all those attached to the deceased.

MARRIED

On the 9th of October, at Sabine Pass, Mr. Fredrick Gorrisen, to Miss Lizzie A. Moore, all of Sabine Pass.

OBITUARY

There are few persons in this community who have not been deeply and sorrowfully affected by the dispensation of Providence which has removed from her earthly sphere, Miss Mary L. Bruton. (Lengthy eulogy follows.)

Whereas this Lodge, through the Secretary of Kaufman Lodge, No. 115, have recently heard of the demise of our much-esteemed and lamented Brother, James McDonald, who is gone to that bourne from whence no traveler has returned.

Therefore,
	Resolved, 1st, That we deeply sympathise with the bereaved widow and orphans of our deceased Brother.
	Resolved, 2d, That the members of McDonald Lodge wear the usual badge of mourning for the space of thirty days, in token of his memory.
	Resolved, 3d, That all the members of this Lodge meet at the Lodge room at 7 o'clock next Sabbath morning, to join in procession with Kaufman Lodge, at the late residence of our deceased Brother, to pay the last tribute of respect to departed worth.
	Resolved, 4th, That the Secretary furnish the family of our departed Brother with a copy of the above resolutions and a copy to the 'Chronicle' for publication.

S. W. KIRK,
R. V. WARRINS
W. L. BOYKIN,   S. W. W. CORKER.
Secretary McDonald Lodge, No. 120.

November 29, 1853

MARRIAGE

There was quite a stir among the colr'd pop'lation Saturday evening by the marriage of Aaron, a "gemman ob color" to Adeline a lady of the same. We were not present at the nuptial ceremonies; but we are informed that "Wiley" "hung up the fiddle and the bow" and did the parson with infinite grace. The bride before leaving the mansion of her mistress was crowned with the bridal wreath by one of our most accomplished ladies. The supper prepared for the occasion is said to have been au fait. The whole scene would have afforded a splendid frountispiece for "Uncle Tom's Cabin," and we have no doubt that Mrs. H. B. Stowe would have gathered a few new and instructive ideas, that would greatly assist her imagination in future attempts to illustrate the domestic institutions of the South.
	We received a very fine package of cake from "Aaron" on Sunday, papered and ribboned after the most approved style,- which will account for the above notice.

OBITUARY

At a called meeting of Rankin Lodge, No. 18, I.O.O.F., held on Friday, the 25th instant, the following Preamble and Resolutions were unanimously adopted;
	Whereas this Lodge has been informed of the death of our well-beloved Brother, M. A. Newton, who departed this life on the 18th inst., in Mansfield, La., Therefore, Resolved, That we deeply sympathise with the family of our deceased Brother, in their Affliction. (Resolutions in usual form follow).

I hereby certify that the foregoing is a true copy from the minutes of the Lodge.   J. M. Seeton,
                         Sec'y Rankin Lodge, No. 18, I.O.O.F.

December 13, 1853

MARRIED

On the 8th inst., near this place, by James Hart, Esq., Mr. William Weaver, to Miss Jane D. Horton.

In Marion, Angelina county, on the 8th inst., by A. C. Caldwell, Esq., Mr. W. B. Hardeman of Washington county, to Miss Mary Curl, of Nacogdoches county.

February 28, 1854

MARRIED

On the 23d inst., by Rev. J. C. Barnett, Mr. A. G. Crouch, of Melrose, to Miss Susan Jones, of Nacogdoches.

March 28, 1854

MARRIED

On the 24th inst., by James Hart, Esq., Mr. Warren C. Harned, to Miss Mary Jane Steward; all of this place.

OBITUARY

Douglass Temple of Honor, No. 6,
March 25, 1854

Whereas it has seemed good in the sight of our Heavenly Parent to call our well-beloved Brother, John A. King, W. G. and member of the social Degree, from this stage of transitory existence, thereby removing from our Temple one of its firm Pillars:
Resolved, That in this dispensation of Providence we are called upon again, in the course of a few short months, to mourn the loss of a much esteemed Brother......... (Usual resolutions follow).
                            Loudon B. Ward,
                            R. E. Kyle,
                            J. R. Clute, Committee

April 18, 1854

MARRIED

At Marcelline, Adams county, Illinois, on 25th March, J. W. DeBall, M.D. late of Douglass, To Miss Hannah A. Ballard, daughter of Dr. Harvey Ballard, of Marcelline.

Of course the happy couple started immediately for Texas.

May 16, 1854

MARRIED

On the 9th inst., by James Hart Esq., Mr. Dan'l F. Coats to Miss Harriet Burrows all of this county.

May 23, 1854

MARRIED

On the 18th instant, by the Rev. Mr. Neris, at the residence of Hon. W. B. Ochiltree, in this place, Gen. J. H. Rogers of Cass county, to Miss C. Ochiltree of Nacogdoches.

We bow our acknowledgments for the bountiful supply of wedding cake, falling to our share. Our best wishes attend the happy couple.

On the 18th instant, by James Hart Esq., Mr. James M. Power to Mrs. Emily Strode, all of this county.

Thanks for the Printers fee. May the newly married couple not only be happy, but become wealthy and power-full; and we earnestly hope, that while the great powers of Europe are exhausting themselves in a war, there may spring up before the small powers, a path Strode with peace.

DIED

On the 16th inst., Eliza Helen Muckleroy, daughter of Jesse H. and Amanda M. Muckleroy, aged fifteen months.

August 15, 1854

DROWNED

Mr. Albert Wells was drowned, near Quitman, Wood County, on the 9th inst.

DIED

In this place, on the 6th inst., after a lingering

illness, Mrs. Tabitha R. Simpson, wife of Wm. P. Simpson, aged 27 years.

In San Augustine, Texas, August 6th, 1854, after a protracted illness, Mrs. Harriet Caroline Berry, consort of Gen. John G. Berry.

August 29, 1854

MARRIED

At the residence of Dr. Wm. Evans, in the vicinity of Marshall, at 8 o'clock on Tuesday morning last, the 8th instant, by the Rev. George Tucker, S. P. Donley, Esq., of Cherokee county, to Miss Judith M. Evans, of Harrison.

In Mount Enterprise, Sunday morning, the 20th inst., by C. P. Matlock, Esq., at the residence of the bride's father, Mr. Cooper B. Nash, Mr. Thomas Henderson, of Henderson county, Texas, and Miss Mary E. Nash. Long may the happy pair live to enjoy happiness in this life;
>And when their days on earth are ended,
>And their life's sands waste away,
>Then, oh then, may they find blended,
>With their hopes, eternal day.   W.G.

At San Augustine, August 3d. by Rev. E. H. Downing, Thomas Smith, Esq., of Henderson, to Miss Susan A. Price, of San Augustine.

DIED

At the residence of her daughter, in Houston county, on the 27th inst., Mrs. Susannah N. White, wife of James T. White, of this place.

FIGHT

A fight occured at Jones' Prairie, in Walker county, on the 9th inst., between two men, named Hawkins and Leighton, in wich the latter was stabbed. Hawkins has fled.

HOMICIDE

We sincerely regret to state that [a man] by the name of W. H. Lowry was [killed] on Monday last, in this place, by T[?] Willingham. Lowry had taken [   ] company with a man by the name [of   ]pree in the outskirts of town, and [on his] return was waylaid, and shot [with a] double-barreled shot-gun. He fell [mortally] wounded, was taken to the office of [Dr.] Roberts where he expired after four [hours] of most

intense suffering. Willingham effected his escape, and although [attempts] have been made to arrest him, is [still] at large. We do not know enough [about] the particulars of the origin of this [regre-]table occurrence, and can only say [that] Willingham was shot at by Lowry [about] eighteen months since, for which ([it is] generally believed) he was killed.
San Augustine Redlander.

October 10, 1854

DROWNED

A youth named Henry Lockhardt, aged about 10 or 12 years, was drowned on Sunday, the 24th inst. He was crossing the Bayou in a skiff, in which was another boy, and a negro, when the skiff capsized. The little fellow was unable to swim and went down; the others swam ashore.

DIED

At the residence of Dr. G. S. Hyde, three miles from Nacogdoches, Mr. James V. Robinson, in the 26th year of his age.

Mr. Robinson emigrated to Texas, about three years since; and up to the period of his protracted illness, of about three months, was a resident of this place. In the hours of health, his gay and generous disposition made him a favorite with a large circle of friends; and in the midst of his sickness, even down to the close of life, it was their pleasure to extend to him those offices of kindness and affection which calm the fevered brow and smooth the dying pillow. Away from the home of his childhood, he died before the golden summers of youth became tinged with the sere of the autumn of life; but yet surrounded by a fond wife and with the prattle of his little one sounding in his ears,- associates of present and former days by his bedside, he passed away from life as calmly as though its light was there to brighten the pathway to the grave.

April 3, 1855

MARRIED

On the 27th inst., by James Hart, Esq., Mr. Victor J. Simpson, to Miss Hariet Arnold, all of this county.

STAGE LINE

Messers. Parmalee & Co's. stage line seems to be well patronized and give great satisfation to travelers. We heard a passenger remark the other evening that it is the best stage line in the Union.

THE NORTHERN STANDARD, CLARKSVILLE, TEXAS

August 20, 1842

MARRIED

On the 4th instant, by Rev. Samuel Corley, Mr. Wm. McAdams to Miss Sarah Turner.
On the 4th instant, by Rev. Samuel Corley, Mr. Isaac Matthews to Miss Mary Turner.
On the 7th instant, by Thomas Willison, Esq., Mr. Robert H. Graham to Miss Minerva Ann Hanks.
On the 9th instant, by A. H. McKenzie, Esq., Mr. James Clark to Miss Nancy Kenner.
On the 9th instant, by the Rev. Samuel Corley, Mr. Chas. Aims to Mrs. Harriet Potter.
On the 9th instant, by the Rev. Samuel Corley, Mr. Montgomery Vaught to Miss Rosanna Land.
On the 11th instant, by the Rev. Samuel Corley, Abner H. McKinzie, Esq., to Mrs. Mary Denton.
The above parties were all of this county.

August 27, 1842

MARRIED

On Thursday evening, by Ulysses Aiguier, Esq., Mr. Thos. F. Bryarly to Mrs. Minerva Ann Oliver, both of this county.
On the 21st instant, by the Rev. Samuel Corley, Mr. John M. Ritchey to Miss Jane J. Sampson, both of this town.
On the 23rd instant, by the Rev. Samuel Corley, Mr. Andrew Vaught to Miss Louisa Wilson, both of Lamar County.

September 3, 1842

MARRIED

On the 17th January, 1842, by Willard Stowell, Esq., Mr. Charles Gardner to Mrs. Sermilia Herley.
On the 11th January, 1842, by John H. Crook, Esq., Mr. Sterling E. Williams to Miss Emeline Roland.
On the 28th February, by Judge Rutherford, Mr. Lee Foster to Mrs. Martha Hogan.
On the 10th February, by Judge Rutherford, Mr. Joshua Morgan to Mrs. Cynthia Bonner.
On the 14th March, by Judge Rutherford, Mr. Alford Freeman to Miss Pamlia Freeman.
On the 20th March, by Judge Rutherford, Mr. James Williams to Mrs. Emeline Fedrick.
On 3rd April, by W. M. Crisp, Esq., Mr. Joseph N. Dornstin to Miss Eliza J. Johnson.

THE NORTHERN STANDARD, CLARKSVILLE, TEXAS

On the 14th April, by John H. Crook, Esq., Mr. John G. Shepert to Miss Rebecca Cherry.

On 14th April, by John H. Crook, Esq., Mr. Atlas Dodd to Miss Rebecca Johnson.

On 23rd April, by B. C. Fowler, Esq., Mr. William McKinney to Miss Emily Leech.

In April, by Isaac J. Nowell, Esq., Mr. Eb'r Freeman to Miss Polly Hutchins.

On 6th June, by Nicholas Maddox, Esq., Mr. John Lane to Miss Rosanna Brown.

On June 30, by James W. Riley, Esq., Mr. Thomas Wideman to Miss Sarah Deck.

On 17th July, by Isaac J. Nowell, Esq., Mr. Erwin Curtis to Miss Nancy J. Williams.

On 25th July, by John H. Crook, Esq., Mr. John D. Black, of Fannin County, to Miss Martha Roland.

On 8th August, by Isaac J. Nowell, Esq., Mr. Lewis M. Snow to Miss Elizabeth Schoonover.

On 9th August, by John A. Dillingham, Esq., Mr. Joseph M. Thomas to Miss Katherine Dalph.

On 8th August, by Isaac J. Nowell, Esq., Mr. William Chisum to Miss Eliza J. Davis.

On 10th August, by John A. Dillingham, Mr. James Dillingham to Miss Angeline Smith.

On 18th August, by Isaac J. Nowell, Esq., Mr. Silas Moore to Miss Harrietta Schoonover.

The above were all of Lamar County.

September 10, 1842

MARRIED

On the 8th instant, by the Rev. Samuel Corley, Mr. Alfred Alking to Miss Mary Ann Row.

September 17, 1842

MARRIED

In this county, on the 15th instant, by John T. Clark, Esq., Mr. W. C. Ingram to Miss Sarah Pope.

October 15, 1842

MARRIED

On the 8th ult., in Lamar County, by George Willison, Esq., Mr. David Bishop to Mrs. Eliza Candell.

On the 20th ult., by J. H. Crook, Esq., Mr. James Graham to Miss Eliza Ann Skidmore.

THE NORTHERN STANDARD, CLARKSVILLE, TEXAS

October 22, 1842

MARRIED

On the 29th ultimo, in Bowie County, by the Hon. James N. Smith, Dr. Lemuel Peters to Miss Elizabeth Heatherly.

October 29, 1842

MARRIED

On the 29th instant, by Thomas Willison, Esq., Mr. Abraham Stallings to Miss Permelia L. Bates, all of this county.

November 5, 1842

MARRIED

On the 8th ult., by the Rev. Alexander Avery, Mr. John W. Reed of Arkansas, to Miss Paralee Gibbons of Lamar County.
On the 12th ult., by William C. Harrison, Esq., Mr. Brent Horne to Miss Martha Ann Doss, of Lamar County.

Out of about one hundred marriages that we have published, since the establishment of the Standard, not one "remembered the Printer!" It shows the degeneracy of the times, and it is a sad example of the "ingratitude of the Republic!" We don't believe that people have cakes and wine now-a-days, at their weddings-alas, for the good old days, the days when the Printer was not forgotten!
The Devil, Loquitur.

November 26, 1842

MARRIED

In this County, on Wednesday evening, the 9th ultimo, by the Rev. J. M. Sampson, Mr. Napoleon Patton to Miss Lucinda Proctor.
In Lamar County, in September last, by N. Maddox, Esq., Mr. Ephraim Williams to Miss America Jackson.
In Lamar County, on the 20th ult., by J. H. Crook, Esq., Mr. Henry Trimble to Miss Jane Graham.
In Lamar County, on the 8th September last, by N. Maddox, Esq., Mr. John T. Bryant to Miss Martha Witherspoon.
In Lamar County, on the 19th of October, by John A. Dillingham, Esq., Mr. William McCoral, of Fannin County, to Miss Martha Ann Smith.

THE NORTHERN STANDARD, CLARKSVILLE, TEXAS

December 10, 1842

MARRIED

On Thursday evening last, by the Rev. Samuel Corley, Mr. Dudley Gillum to Miss Patsey Mason, all of this place.

December 17, 1842

DIED

In Lamar County, on the 4th Nov., 1842, Mrs. Jane Allen, wife of Wm. Allen, aged 33 years.

January 7, 1843

MARRIED

On the .. October, in Lamar County, by John A. Dillingham, Esq., Mr. William McCoral to Miss Martha Ann Smith.
On the 1st Dec., in Lamar County, by A. N. Hopkins, Esq., Mr. Merett Brandon to Miss Elizabeth E. Finley.
On the 11th December, in Lamar County, by A. N. Hopkins, Esq., Mr. James Rodgers, late of the state of Alabama, to Miss Martha Birdwell.

January 14, 1843

MARRIED

On the 13th instant, by Judge B. ..... Esq., Mr. Simon Wagley to Mrs. Martha Wells, all of this county.

DIED

On Friday the 16th instant, Fanny M. Russell, consort of Charles W. Russell, aged 37 years.
The subject of this brief notice has heretofore occupied a large share of attention as the celebrated Mrs. Pritchard of the Theatre Royal, and of the principal Theatres of the United States.
Mrs. Russell had been amongst us but a short time previous to her death, and during that period, although suffering under an acute and painful disease, which has finally terminated her course, she bore with a noble fortitude the change of life and circumstances with which she was surrounded. Of her talents, as an able and faithful delineator of the more stirring scenes and passions of life, it is useless now to speak. She has left behind her name and fame that the notaries of Thespis will long delight to cherish, and while the remembrance of what she has been, is

forced upon the memory, the words of the enthusiast may well be applied here, "non omnis moriar." (lengthy eulogy follows)

January 28, 1843

MARRIED

On Thursday evening last, by the Rev. Mr. Duke, Mr. John Cameron of Lamar County, to Miss Lunette Deen, of Red River.

April 6, 1843

MARRIED

In Lamar County, on the 5th March, by the Rev. William Brackeen, Mr. Live Goins to Mrs. Margaret Whorton.
In Lamar County on 7th March, by the Rev. Ramsey Potts, Mr. John McMinn to Miss Eveline S. Majors.
In Lamar County on the 14th March, by A. N. Hopkins, Esq., Mr. Greenbery Walding to Miss Sarah Harvick.

April 20, 1843

NOTICE

The Marshall Review has lately changed hands, and the name of L. A. W. Laird, appears as editor and proprietor.

July 27, 1843

MARRIED

On the 2nd inst., by Thos. Willison, Esq., Mr. William Brown to Mrs. Elizabeth McAnier, all of this county.
On the 20th inst., by Thos. Willison, Esq., Mr. Francis L. Blanton to Miss Mary McAnier, all of this county.

October 28, 1843

OBITUARY

Departed this life at the residence of her husband, in Bowie County, Texas, on the 19th day of September, Mrs. Sarah Whitaker, consort of Wilis Whitaker, Esq., in the 33rd year of her life.

THE NORTHERN STANDARD, CLARKSVILLE, TEXAS

November 4, 1843

MARRIED

On Thursday the 2nd instant, by the Rev. James Sampson, Amos Morrill, Esq., a native of Salisbury, Mass., to Miss Miranda A. Dickson of this County.

November 25, 1843

OBITUARY

Died at his residence at Savanah, 12 miles below town, on Thursday the 21st inst., Col. James Titus, the late Senator from this district, aged 68 years.

Col. Titus was born in Virginia Dec. 10th, 1775, removed when very young to Tennessee, near Nashville, from there to Alabama, where he was several times a member of the legislature, and from there he removed to Shelby County, Tennessee, whence he came to this country.....

December 2, 1843

MARRIED

In Lamar County, on the 1st Nov., 1843, by the Rev. J. W. P. McKenzie, Dr. C.C. Cooper to Miss Catherine Harmon.

In Lamar County, on the 5th Nov., 1843, by A. N. Hopkins, Esq., Col. Lindley Johnson to Miss Everly C. Merrill.

In Lamar County, on the 9th Nov., 1843, by the Rev. Sam Corley, Mr. J. W. Tomlinson, of Red River County, to Miss Pamelia Jane Gibbons.

February 3, 1844

MARRIED

On the 22 ultimo, by Thomas Willison, Esq., Mr. Joseph Cartwright to Sarah Caroline Wilkins, all of this County.

On the 7th inst., by John A. Dillingham, Esq., Mr. Nelson Staats, of Red River County, to Miss Nancy W. Dillingham, of Lamar County.

March 9, 1844

MARRIED

At the residence of Philip Duty, Esq., near town, on Friday the 22nd Feb., by the Rev. Sam'l Corley, Dr. Enos S. Look, of this town, to Miss Mary Duty.

THE NORTHERN STANDARD, CLARKSVILLE, TEXAS

In Lamar County, on the 19th January, by the Rev. Wm. Bracham, Mr. James Wimberly, to Miss Cinthia Hart.

On the 28th January, by the Rev. J. W. P. McKenzie, Mr. Charles A. Warfield, to Miss Martha P. Hamilton.

On the 8th Feb., By Jacob Lysday, Esq., Dr. H. G. McDonald to Mrs. Sarah Turner.

March 16, 1844

MARRIED

On Sunday evening last, by the Rev. Mr. Corley, Mr. Hugh F. Young to Miss Angeline Alexander, all of this county.

April 17, 1844

DIED

At his father's residence, near this place, on Thursday the 11th inst., John Johns Vining, in the 24th year of his age... His father being the Clerk of the District Court for this County, he, as his deputy for the last three years, has performed mostly the duties appertaining to that office.
(The Huntsville (Ala.) Democrat and Memphis (Tenn.) papers please copy.)

May 8, 1844

MARRIED

On the 14th day of April, 1844, at Jordan's Mills, by W. J. Hamilton, Esq., Mr. W. H. Benton, recently from Tennessee, to Miss Ellenor Jordan, daughter of Levi Jordan, Esq.

At the same time and place, Mr. John Millstead, to Miss Susan Starnes, daughter of Mr. Aaron Starnes, all of Red River County.

May 29, 1844

MARRIED

On the evening of the 23 inst., by the Rev. J. W. P. McKenzie, Mr. L. D. VanDyke of Bowie County, to Miss Adelia F. West, daughter of Major Edward West of this county, at his residence near town.

In Lamar County, by the Hon. John A. Rutherford, on the 5th May Mr. A. B. Robertson, to Miss Rachel Juell.

By A. N. Hopkins, Esq., on the 18th of March last, Mr. D. O. Norton, to Miss Lydia A. Crabtree.

By A. N. Hokes, Esq., on the 19th of March last, Mr. David R. Wood to Mary Hobbs.

THE NORTHERN STANDARD, CLARKSVILLE, TEXAS

By J. H. Crook, Esq., on the 2nd March, Mr. E. Thompson, to Miss Rhoda Payne.
By J. H. Crook, Esq., on the 19th April last, Mr. John Gregg, [Grogg?] to Miss Lucretia Thompson.
By L. V. More, Esq., on the 7th April, Mr. Henry Robertson, to Miss Nancy Blankinship.
By J. H. Crook, Esq., on 22nd April, Mr. L. Ratton to Miss Eliza Cooper, all of Lamar County.
By Lovell Coffman, Esq., on the 16th inst., Mr. Thomas Spears, to Miss Jane Raney, all of Red River County.
By the same on the 28th inst., Mr. James Pairan, to Miss Arena Clampet, all of Pine Creek.

June 26, 1844

MARRIED

On the 23 inst., by Thos. Willison, Esq., Mr. James Heath to Miss Rosetta Langford.
On Thursday last, by the Hon. Wm. B. Stout, Wm. W. Fullerton, to Miss Martha Gum, all of this county.

July 4, 1844

DIED

In Trinity County, on Thursday, the 21st of June, Mr. Samuel Browning formerly of Louisville, Ky., and since then of the city of Austin, in the 43rd year of his age. Mr. Browning was one of the original contractors for the first Trinity Colony, under the grant of 1841. He settled in it when it was a wilderness, had remained in it, and administered to its interests under all its vicisitudes, and at last after having endured much privation, and seen hundreds come and go, and the Colony at one time, with only sixteen families left in it, out of the large number who had ventured, but shrunk away again, from the hardships, and hazards of a wild country, he lived long enough to see the success of the enterprize, and the securement of the contract. When he died, there were sixteen families more, within its limits, than were required to comply with the terms of the contract. Mr. Browning was an amiable, worthy man, and has left a family to mourn his loss.

July 24, 1844

DIED

Major Edward B. Ely, agent for contractors of Trinity Colony, died of bilious fever, at the residence of Mr. Kenner, in the Colony, on Sunday 7th, July, after an illness of 21 days. He had the medical aid of Dr. ... and the day before... [illegible]

THE NORTHERN STANDARD, CLARKSVILLE, TEXAS

August 21, 1844

OBITUARY

Died of acute gastritis on his plantation in the Southern District of Red River County, Noah Lilly, Esq., in the 74th year of age. He was born in Martin County, North Carolina in 1771, emigrated to Tennessee at an early day from where he came to Texas in 1837.

He was a kind and indulgent parent, an honored, benevolent citizen, and has left a large circle of friends and connections to mourn his loss...

September 4th, 1844

OBITUARY

Died in Bowie County, on the 22nd ultimo, after a very short illness, Alfred Harris, aged about 12 years, the youngest son of R. C. Harris, Esq....

October 2, 1844

MARRIED IN LAMAR COUNTY

On the 7th of December, 1843, by J. T. Harmon, Esq., Mr. L. J. Crook, to Mrs. Matilda Harmon.

On the 29th March, 1844, by ...., Mr. Murheh [?] to Mrs. R. Hunt.

On the 18th March, 1844, by A. N. Hopkins, Esq., Mr. D. O. Norton to Miss Lydia Crabtree.

On the 19th March, by A. N. Hopkins, Esq., David R. Wood to Miss Mary Hobbs.

On 2nd March, by John H. Crook, Esq., Mr. Edward Thompson to Mrs. Rhoda Page.

On the 18th April, by John H. Crook, Esq., Mr. John Gregg to Miss Lucretia Thompson.

On the 7th April, by L. V. More, Esq., Henry Robertson to Nancy Blankenship.

On the 22nd April, by J. H. Crook, Mr. Littleton Ratton to Mrs. A. Eliza Cooper.

On 5th May, by J. A. Rutherford, Chief Justice, Mr. A. R. Robertson to Miss Rachel Jewell.

On the 3rd April, by Jacob Wilson, Esq., Mr. John H. Burns [?] to Miss Malinda Ratton.

On the 15th May, by J. H. Crook, Mr. Jas. Kendal to Miss...

On the 6th June, by A. N. Hopkins, Mr. Silas Eavins to Susan Schoolcraft.

On the 2nd May, by J. W. Riley, Esq., Mr. Harvey Skiles to Miss Martha Parker.

On the 9th May, by Lucas Buford, Esq., Mr. Isaac Hobbs to Mrs. Martha Turner.

On the 30th June, by the Rev. J. Shook, Mr. C. R. B. Anderson to Miss Nancy Askins.

On the 18th July, by J. A. Dillingham, Esq., Mr. Granville Davis to Miss Nancy Taylor.

On the 11th July, by L. V. Moore, Joseph Sach [?] Esquire, to Mrs. Elisabeth P. Wortham.

On the 31st July, by the Rev. W. Brackem, Mr. Reuben Williams to Mrs. Polly Barnett.

[Other entries illegible.]

DIED

At his residence four miles east of Paris, Lamar County, on the ..., of ..., Enoch Crow, Esquire, of congestive fever.

October 30, 1844

MARRIED

On the 16th instant, by his Honor, Chief Justice Wm. B. Stout, Mr. James M. Sharp, to Miss Mary Dean, daughter of the late Edward M. Dean, all of this County.

DIED

At his father's residence in Lamar County, on the 16th inst., George W. Mabane, of consumption.

December 4, 1844

MARRIED

On the 3rd Nov., 1844, by L. Coffman, Esq., Mr. James Henderson to Mrs. Sarah Kuykendall, all of this County.

January 16, 1845

DIED

In Sevier County, Arkansas, about the 22nd of December last, while on his way to this country, Maj. John Starkey, late of St. Clair County, Illinois, aged 52 years.
(Illinois paper please copy.)

In this town, on the 6th inst., Mrs. Electia Angelina Young, Wife of Hugh F. Young, Esq., aged 22 years.

THE NORTHERN STANDARD, CLARKSVILLE, TEXAS

June 21, 1845

DIED

In this town, on Sunday evening last, of colera morbus, Matilda, infant daughter of Dr. E. S. Look.

November 12, 1845

DIED

In this town, on the 23rd September, of apoplexy, Mr. Wm. Donaho, aged 48 years. The deceased was a native of Madison County, Kentucky, and had lived in this place since 1839.

Near Savannah, 12 miles from Clarksville, on the 16th instant, of ulcerated sore throat, Mrs. Ann W. Billingsly, wife of Capt. Jesse Billingsly, aged 21 years.

In this town, on yesterday evening, about 4 o'clock, of typhus fever, Rufus K. Clark, Esq., aged 21 years, son of Robert Clark, of Bedford County, Tennessee.

November 19, 1845

DIED

On the 16th of this inst., 8 miles south of Clarksville, of scarlet fever, Mary Helen, infant daughter of W. B. and Matilda C. Stout, aged eight months and one day.

November 26, 1845

DIED

In this county on the 21st inst., eight miles south of Clarksville, of scarlet fever, Sarah Isabella, infant daughter of W. B. and Matilda C. Stout, aged one year, eleven months and fourteen days.

December 24, 1845

MARRIED

On last evening, the 23rd inst., by the Rev. Samuel Corley, Hon. Ballard C. Bagby, to Miss Amanda Bagby, daughter of Major John A. Bagby, all of this County.

THE NORTHERN STANDARD, CLARKSVILLE, TEXAS

May 27, 1846

MARRIED

In this town, on Thursday the 21st inst., by the Rev. Washington Fields, Mr. John Brackney to Miss Nancy O. Collins.

June 3, 1846

MARRIED

On the 26th of May, by the Rev. James Sampson, Mr. John Carter to Mrs. Mary Ann Dinwiddie.

July 15, 1846

DIED

In this County on 12th June last, of consumption, T. L. D. Collins, son of Mrs. Diana Collins.
If her son, John W. Collins, should see this notice, he will understand that his mother is in a strange land needing his assistance.

August 8, 1846

DIED

In this town on the 23rd of July, John J. Montgomery, aged forty-six years, formerly of Giles County, Tennessee.

August 22, 1846

DIED

At the residence of Edward West, Esq., near town, on Sunday last, suddenly, from a violent kick by a horse, over the region of the heart, Charles Wooldridge De Morse, son of Charles and Lodoiska C. DeMorse, aged six years, eight months, and eleven days old.

September 5, 1846

DIED

In Lamar County, on the 9th of August, of bilious fever, Laura Isadora, infant daughter of Cap. R. and Mary B. Holman, aged seven months and eleven days. (Washington [Arkansas] Telegraph please copy.)

THE NORTHERN STANDARD, CLARKSVILLE, TEXAS

September 26, 1846

DIED

At Jonesborough, Red River County, on the 20th inst., Mrs. Jane Chandler Gill, consort of Wm. H. Gill, in the 30th year of her age.

On Saturday the 19th inst., of congestive chill, Harriet Sophronia Jane, wife of Wm. M. Bowers, aged 15 years, eleven months and eleven days. She left a husband and a little baby, with many friends to mourn her loss...

October 10, 1846

DIED

In Lamar County, on the 17th ult., Mrs. Lizie [?] Hilburn [?], consort of Mathias [?] Hilburn [?] aged 74 years. [Amost illegible, eulogy follows.]

October 31, 1846

MARRIED

In this town, on Tuesday evening the 20th inst., by the Rev. Mr. Corley, Mr. Gilbert Ragen, to Miss Mary Donoho, all of this place.

We were waited upon, on Thursday night last, by Mr. Ingles Oliver, of the Clarksville Bakery, who brought with him, as an earnest of the compliments of the bridegroom, which he presented in due form, a large frosted cake, decked out in a style of superior magnificence accompanied with various contingencies of wine, conserves, fruits, and candies.

November 7, 1846

MARRIED

By the Rev. James Graham, in Lamar County, G. W. Lovejoy, to Miss Highfill(?)

By the same, on the same day at 7 o'clock p.m., Wm. H. Newland to Miss Amanda C. Houndshell, all of Lamar County.

DIED

In this town, on Friday morning the 30th ult., Miss Martha Maggie Robbson [?] aged 15 years and seven months.

On Friday the 23 ult., at Ringwood, Bowie County, Sarah D. Clark, daughter of Mrs. Gordon of Clarksville, aged 14 years and two months.

THE NORTHERN STANDARD, CLARKSVILLE, TEXAS

On the 20th of October, Mrs. Sarah H. Boyce, consort of Dr. William Boyce, at his residence in Bowie County. [Lengthy eulogy follows.]

We learn with regret, the death of Mr. Davis Bell, one of the Volunteers who went out at the call of the Governor, from this immediate neighborhood. He died at Bucksnort on the Brazos, on his return home. He was an amiable and estimable young man.

December 5, 1846

DIED

At Savannah, Red River County, Texas, November 13th, 1846, in the 59th year of her age, Mrs. Rebecca Titus, widow of Col. James Titus. She was born in Davidson County, Tennessee, August 3rd, 1788, daughter of Col. R. Edmonson of said County and State. (The Memphis Appeal will please copy.)

Departed this life on the morning of the 15th of November, at the residence of his son-in-law, Dr. Lemuel Peters, in Boston, Bowie County, Texas, Col. Thomas Heatherly, in the forty sixth year of his age after a protracted illness. Mr. H. was a native of Kentucky, and emigrated to this country in the spring of 1842, since which time he had the misfourtune to lose the partner of his bosom. He has left several children to mourn his loss. (The Richmond, Ky., papers will please copy this.)

December 19, 1846

MARRIED

On the 5th February last, by A. Nevill, Esq., Martin G. Jones, to Mrs. Elizabeth Millsap.

On the 26th October last, by the Rev. Mr. Webbs, James M. Learza, to Miss Margaret A. Stewart.

On the 4th November last, by the Hon. Thomas S. Burns, William Johnson, to Miss Sarah C. Ward.

On the 14th November last, by Thos. Willison, Esq., West W. Hickey, Esq., to Miss Elizabeth Keith, all of Titus County.

In Lamar County on the 13th last, by Wm. H. Wynn, Esq., John Wheat to Miss Catherine W. Stewart.

DIED

In Lavaca County, Texas, 5th inst., Mr. Montreville [?] C. Rountree, aged about 33 years [suicide]. His father lives near Hickory Grove, Warren County, Mississippi. [More eulogy.]

THE NORTHERN STANDARD, CLARKSVILLE, TEXAS

December 24, 1846

OBITUARY

Departed this life on Saturday evening the 12th inst., Mrs. Rebecca Dale in the 21st year of her age, having a husband and three small children to mourn a loss that can not be repaired this side of heaven. Sister Dale was baptised into the fellowship of the First United Baptist Church, Clarksville, in June 43.

January 5, 1847

DIED

In this town, on Friday the 31st ult. of pleurisy, Samuel S. Smith, Esq., aged 44 years. The corpse was taken to the family residence on Pine Creek, and was attended to the edge of town by the Masonic fraternity, with the usual honors.

-- -- --

Departed this life on the 29th inst., at his residence in Bowie County, the Honorable Richard Ellis. Judge Ellis had been in a feeble situation for several years, yet his death was very sudden and unexpected. On the day of his death, his son, who had been absent from home several weeks, remained with him all day. In the evening his son went out, to give some orders, and in his absence, the Judge who was lying on the bed at the time, and supposed to be asleep, arose, and was seen by servants to walk out in the passage, and return to his room by the fire, where by some means, his clothes which were of combustible material, took fire, and although the alarm was immediately given, and every possible assistance was rendered by his son and servants, his death was almost instantaneous.

Judge Ellis was born the 14th February, 1781, in the State of Virginia. At an early age he read law in Richmond, Virginia, in the office of Wirt & Wickham, and practised Law for several years, in his native state. He emigrated to Alabama at an early date, was a member of the Convention that framed the Constitution for that State, afterwards elected Judge of the District and Supreme Court, which office he filled for seven years, with much credit to himself and satisfaction to the State. He then moved to West Tennessee and was appointed President of the first meeting held at Memphis to connect a rail road from that point to the Eastern cities.

He emigrated to Texas in the year of 1834 and in 1836 was elected a member to the Convention that framed the Constitution of the Republic of Texas, appointed President of that Body, afterwards elected to the Senate and made President of that Body.

Judge Ellis, rendered many valuable and distinguished services to the Republic of Texas in its infancy, and should

ever be remembered by the country. His death will be deeply felt by the community and his memory cherished by his many friends and acquaintances. He was a kind and affectionate parent, a humane and indulgent master, and kind neighbor. He has left a son, and a daughter, and a large circle of friends and acquaintances to mourn his irreparable loss.
[communicated]

-- -- --

On Saturday night last, of pneumonia, in the 39th year of his age, Dr. John S. Peters... The deceased was a Mason. Dr. Peters was a native of Clarksville, Tennessee, received his medical education at Philadelphia where he graduated in 1833, and subsequently practised his profession in Courtland, Ala., whence he moved to Bowie County, Texas, in 1837, and thence to this Town in 1846. His constitution had been impaired years since by a too rigid attention to medical practice, and living in unhealthy situations, and he had looked forward for some years, to just such an attack as finally carried him off.

-- -- --

Died in the Clarksville Hotel on Friday the 1st inst. of Pleuresy, Samuel Simpson Smith, Esq., of this County, in the 47 year of his age. Major Smith was a native of Bascombe County, North Carolina, from which place he moved to the Western part of Tennessee. In 1836 he immigrated to Texas and settled upon Pine Creek, about 20 miles from this, which was his home until his decease. He left his family to attend the Court now in session, and only two days previous to his burial was in his seat as a Juror...

Major Smith was a Mason of high rank, and his corpse was attended to his residence by a large number of his brethren, of that order. Peace be with his ashes.
[communicated]

January 30, 1847

DIED

At her residence near Clarksville, of inflammation of the brain, on the 19th inst., Mrs. Ann G., daughter of Fremon and Martha Smith, and Consort of Samuel A. Richey, aged 28 years and 17 days.

Sister Richey was born in Wilson County, Tenn. near Sisterville, professed religion at Moriah Camp-Ground in the fall of 36, and attached herself to the C. P. Church, in the communion of which she lived and died a respected member... She has left her aged parents, bereaved husband and infant daughter, many relatives and friends to mourn their loss...

THE NORTHERN STANDARD, CLARKSVILLE, TEXAS

February 13, 1847

MARRIED

On Saturday, Jan. 3rd, at Richland, Navarro Co., Dr. W. N. Anderson, to Miss Susanna Louisa Dixson.

February 20, 1847

MARRIED

At the residence of Dr. G. H. Wootten in the Town of Clarksville, on Thursday evening the 11th inst., by the Rev. J. W. McKenzie, Dr. Jas. W. Strawn, of Florence, Geo., to Miss Ann E. Wootten, daughter of Mr. Lemuel Wootten of Millidgeville, Geo.
In this Town on Wednesday morning last, by the Rev. J.W.P. McKenzie, J. K. Oliver, Esq., to Miss Mary A. Chattfield, all of this place.

DIED

At his residence in Bowie County, Texas, on the 4th inst., of hemorrhage, Randolph C. Harris, aged 42 years and four months.
Mr. Harris emigrated to this Country in 1837 from South Alabama.

March 6, 1847

MARRIED

At the residence of Mr. A. Ellis in Bowie County, on the evening of the 22nd ult. by the Rev. Sam'l Corley, J. W. Latimer, Esq. of this Town, to Miss Lucy M. Jordan of Bowie County.

March 27, 1847

MARRIED

On the 24th February by the Rev. P. W. Holts, Mr. J. W. Mork to Mrs. M. Duvall.
On the 2nd day of March, by Judge Latimer, Mr. Joel D. Webb to Miss Isabella Simmons.
On the 4th of March, by Rev. P. W. Hobbs, Mr. Hill I. Allen to Mrs. Anurina Ann Adams... all of Lamar County.

THE NORTHERN STANDARD, CLARKSVILLE, TEXAS

April 1, 1847

OBITUARY

Departed this life, March 22, 1847, Mary Julia, daughter of J. W. and Susan L. Sims, of Red River County, Texas, aged 13 years, 10 months and 23 days. Mary Julia professed religion in her eleventh year...

April 8, 1847

MARRIED

On the 30th ult., by Rev. James Graham, Dr. W. T. F. Coles, to Miss Martha A. Bourland, all of Lamar County.

April 15, 1847

MARRIED

On Thursday evening the 8th instant, at the residence of Col. Johnson Kemp, by the Rev. John Carr, Dr. John McDonough, to Mrs. Malinda Colbert... all of the Choctaw Nation.

May 13, 1847

DIED

On the 29th April, 1847, at his residence at Pine Bluffs, Red River County, Texas, of Typhus Fever, Mr. Joseph Mather, a native of Ireland, but for a number of years a resident of this county.   (New Orleans papers will please copy.)

May 26, 1847

MARRIED

On Tuesday evening the 20th inst., by the Rev. J. W. Fields, the Rev. F. H. Black, A. M. of East Texas Conf., to Miss Odessa F. Swanson of Harrison [?] County, Texas.

June 9, 1847

MARRIED

At Savannah, Red River County, on Thursday evening the 2nd inst., Dr. T. F. Titus of Clarksville, to Miss Sarah M. Brown, formerly of Knoxville, Tenn.

THE NORTHERN STANDARD, CLARKSVILLE, TEXAS

June 23, 1847

MARRIED

In this Town, on the 13th inst., by the Rev. J. W. P. McKenzie, Stephen D. Raney to Miss Mary Russell.

At Pine Bluffs, Red River County, on Thursday the 17th inst., by Marcus G. Settle, Esq., Joseph J. Smith to Mrs. Mary K. Ryder.

DIED

At Monterey, Mexico, on the 26th of April, Wm. W. Vining, aged 28 years, son of Wade H. and Martha Vining of this vicinity.

August 11, 1847

DIED

At Laredo, Texas, about the 1st of June, John R. Bedfort, Esq., formerly of this Town, and originally from Boone County, Missouri.

August 21, 1847

DIED

At her late residence in Paris, Texas, on Monday the 9th inst., after a painful sickness of 15 days, Mrs. Mary Malvina Doss, daughter of Reuben W. and Lucinda H. Reynolds, and consort of Benjamin H. Doss, aged 21 years, 8 months and 3 days.

The deceased has left an only son, and a long list of friends and relatives.

September 11, 1847

MARRIED

On Thursday evening the 9th inst., by Rev'd. Jas. Sampson, Col. A. R. Dickson to Miss Elmina Adams, daughter of Mr. Jesse Adams, all of this vicinity.

DIED

In Clarksville, on the 1st of September, Buena Vista, infant daughter of Lucetta and William Trimble, Esq., aged seventeen months and two days.

THE NORTHERN STANDARD, CLARKSVILLE, TEXAS

At his residence in Lamar County, on the 12th of August, 1847 in the 29th year of his age, Col. Zachariah B. Miller.

December 25, 1847

DIED

At her residence in Red River County, Texas, on the 16th inst., Mrs. Malinda K. Henderson, consort of Col. L. D. Henderson, in the 30th year of her age, leaving a husband and six children to mourn her loss... Mrs. Henderson was a daughter of Col. David Hardin, formerly of Kentucky, and late of Mississippi. (The Holly Springs papers will please copy.)

NOTICE

On Sunday the 26th Dec., inst., the funeral Sermon of Mrs. Mary Jane Martin, consort of Col. B. H. Martin, will be preached at the Presbyterian Church in Clarksville, by the Rev. J. W. P. McKenzie, assisted by the Rev. James Sampson.

January 8, 1848

NOTICE

We are authorized to announce John H. Duke as a candidate for Sheriff of Red River County, at the next election.

April 22, 1848

DIED

In Clarksville, on the 6th of March, of Pneumonia, Mrs. Eliza Durfee, consort of Chas. Durfee, aged 22 years... She has left behind her an infant child and one other, the partner of her life...

June 10, 1848

DIED

Departed this life, at his residence in Bowie County, on the 20th May, Littleton W. House. Mr. House was a native of middle Tennessee, born in Rutherford County, in the year 1810. He has left an affectionate wife and numerous friends to mourn his loss. (The Murfreesboro, Tenn. papers, please copy.)

THE NORTHERN STANDARD, CLARKSVILLE, TEXAS

June 17, 1848

MARRIED

On Wednesday evening last, by the Rev. A. ..., P. Smith, Esq., to Miss Sarah Henderson, daugther of Col. L. D. Henderson, of this city. (Holly Springs papers, please copy.)

June 24, 1848

DIED

At his residence in Brenham, Washington County, on Tuesday, the 16th inst., Thos. Johnson, Esq., late Solicitor in that District, leaving an interesting family, and a large circle of friends to mourn his loss.

The deceased was well known as formerly one of the District Judges of the State, and subsequently the Editor of the National Vindicator. He enjoyed the reputation of being a very honest man. As District Attorney he was a vigorous and powerful prosecutor.

In Paris, Lamar County, on the 20th inst., Cap. Geo. W. Jewell.

MARRIED

On Wednesday evening last, at the residence of Jas. J. Ward, Esq., in Red River County, By John A. Bagby, Esq., Mr. Henry Smith to Mrs. Mary D. Ward.

August 5, 1848

MARRIED

On Thursday evening inst., by the Rev. Sam'l Corley, Mr. J. H. B. Dinwiddie, to Miss Sarah Jane Gilliam, daughter of James Gilliam, Esq., all of this county.

OBITUARY

Died at Holly Springs, Miss., on the 4th of July, Miss Sarah Darnall, aged 28 years.

The deceased lady, was for some years a resident of Clarksville, and had lately gone to Mississippi, in the hope that change of climate, and travelling would loosen the grip of a mortal disease, which for years had laid the weight of a heavy hand upon her...

September 2, 1848

MARRIED

At Dallas on Tuesday, August 15th by William Heard, Esq., Mr. U. Matthiessen of Paris Texas, to Miss Josephine A., daughter of J. B. McDermott, of Dallas County, Texas.

OBITUARY

Died at the residence of Mrs. Martha Runnels on the 9th inst., Mrs. Zerikia Runnels, consort of Mr. Edward Runnels of Bowie County. The deceased was the daugther of the late Col. Heatherly of Lamar, a native of Madison County, Ky. She left a Husband and infant.

September 23, 1848

DIED

In Paris, Lamar County, Texas, on the 2nd inst., Antonia Coles Fowler, the only daughter of B. C. and Mary A. Fowler, aged 1 year, 11 months and 22 days.

September 30, 1848

MARRIED

On Thursday the 24th inst., by the Rev. Sam Corley, Col. Richard Peters to Miss Elizabeth Ann Beaty, daughter of the late Robert E. Beaty, all of this county.

On the 14th inst., in Titus County, by John D. ..., Mr. James H. Keith to Miss Jane O'...

November 4, 1848

DIED

In this town, on the 24th October, of Congestive fever, Mr. John Thom, aged 40 years.

The deceased had been a resident of this place for several years, and was in all relations he bore to his fellow men a good citizen and a strictly honest man.

He was buried by his associates, the Sons of Temperance, with the ceremonials of the Order.

December 23, 1848

DIED

On the 18th inst., at the age of three years,

THE NORTHERN STANDARD, CLARKSVILLE, TEXAS

Josephine, youngest daughter of Col. L. D. Henderson, of this vicinity.

January 13, 1849

MARRIED

On Tuesday night last, at the residence of Philip Duty, Esq., near town, by the Rev. Sam'l Corley, Alexander J. Russell, Esq., to Miss Ann Duty.

January 27, 1849

MARRIED

On the 24th December, at Porter's Bluffs, by Wm. Spelling, Esq., Clinton W. Winkler, to Mrs. Louisa Smith, all of Navarro County.
In Clarksville, on Thursday evening, the 25th inst., by the Rev'd. A. E. Clements, Joshua Fuqua, Esq., to Miss Catharine Ribble, all of this county.

February 10, 1849

DIED

In this Town, on Tuesday night last, Mrs. Lodoika C. DeMorse, wife of the editor of this paper, aged twenty-nine years and twenty one days.

February 17, 1849

MARRIED

By L. Coffman, Esq., Mr. S. P. Greenman to Miss Elizabeth Lea on the 1st day of February, 1849, all of this county.
At Waltooga Hall, Grayson Co., on the 1st inst., by the Rev. Provine, Majr. Thomas G. Murphy to Miss Frances Suttonfield.

March 3, 1849

DIED

In Pontotoc, Mississippi, on the 10th December last, Mr. David C. Edge, a resident of Fannin County. The deceased left a widow in this state to mourn his loss.

THE NORTHERN STANDARD, CLARKSVILLE, TEXAS

March 10, 1849

OBITUARY

Died in Clarksville, about one o'clock on the morning of the 7th March, 1849, Miss Isabella F. Russell, in the seventeenth year of her age.

April 28, 1849

DIED

In this Town, on Wednesday morning last, of Spasmatic Croup, George, infant son of Dr. George and Isabella Gordon.

May 19, 1849

MARRIED

In this city, on Thursday the 15th of March, by the Rev. Dr. Lapsley, Mr. A. M. Alexander, of Texas, and Miss Josephine King, of Burkesville, Ky. [Nashville Gazette.]

In this town [Clarksville], on Thursday evening last, by the Rev. John Anderson, Capt. Henry Gooding, to Miss Letitia E. Talbot, all of this place.

A SAD AFFAIR

In Rusk, Cherokee County, on Thursday the 19th inst., Dr. Rains and Dr. McKay... quarreled and McKay was killed. [Austin ? Statesman.]

June 9, 1849

DIED

In this county on the 4th inst., Elizabeth, the wife of Thomas Lynch, daughter of William and Cynthia Welch, aged 23 years.
She left a husband and two tender offsprings to mourn her loss...

In Hopkins County, on the 27th March, of Inflamation of the Brain, Elizabeth Starkey, aged 19 years, formerly of St. Clair County, Illinois.

June 30, 1849

MARRIED

At the residence of Col. L. M. James, in this county,

THE NORTHERN STANDARD, CLARKSVILLE, TEXAS

on Wednesday evening, the 20th inst., by the Rev. Samuel Corley, J. A. N. Murray, Esq., to Miss Amelia M. James.

July 14, 1849

MARRIED

On Sunday the 24th ult., by the Rev. Nathan Stook, Dr. Calvin C. Cooper, to Miss Amanda, youngest daughter of Colonel John T. Harmon, all of Lamar County.

On Wednesday the 27th ult., by the Rev. John McKee, William Merrick, Esq., to Miss Mary J., daughter of Colonel James Bourland, both of Lamar County.

On the same day, by the Rev. Samuel Corley, Isaiah W. Wells, Esq., of Pine Bluffs, to Miss Sarah, daughter of Major William Tinnin, of Lamar County.

July 28, 1849

DIED

In this Town, on Thursday last, Wm. G., infant child of Eliza A. and Wm. S. Todd.

August 11, 1849

DIED

In this vicinity on the 6th instant, of Congestive fever, Elizabeth Welch, consort of James Welch. She left three tender offsprings to suffer the loss of an affectionate mother, and a husband to mourn the loss of a worthy companion...

September 1, 1849

DIED

In this vicinity, on Tuesday the 21st ultimo, Mrs. Sophia T. Young, wife of Gen. W. C. Young, and daughter of the late Michael Gleavos of Davidson county, Tennessee, aged 34 years. The deceased was the mother of seven children, who are left to mourn the loss of a devoted parent...

MARRIED

On Wednesday evening, the 22nd instant, by the Hon. John T. Mills, Wm. H. Millwee, Esq., of Paris, Texas, to Miss Martha Clack, of Marshall Co., Alabama.

Married on the 16th instant, at the residence of David Rainey, Esq., near town, by the Rev. Wm. Duke, Judge

THE NORTHERN STANDARD, CLARKSVILLE, TEXAS

Hugh F. Young, Chief Justice of this county, to Miss Sarah Rainey.

December 28, 1849

MARRIED

At the residence of John Jackson, Esq., near Town, on Tuesday evening the 25th inst., by Rev. J. W. P. McKenzie, Mr. Wm. P. Saufley, to Miss Eliza Crittenden.

In this Town, on Tuesday night, the 9th of Oct. by the Rev. J. W. P. McKenzie, Mr. Charles Durfee, to Miss Matilda Dew.

In the vicinity, on Tuesday evening, the 16th October, at the residence of Maj. Edward West, by the Rev. J. W. P. McKenzie, Wm. P. Cornelius, Esq., to Miss Arabella West.

At St. Luke's Church, Philadelphia on Thursday, Aug. 16th, by the Rev. D. Washburn, A. M., Commodore E. W. Moore, commander of the late Texas Navy, to Emma, daughter of the late William T. Stockton, of Rosborough, Texas.

OBITUARY

Ann Jones, aged four years, daughter of the Editor of this paper, staying at the residence of Mr. John Jackson, Esq., near town, playing with fire, on the evening of the 18th inst., about dark, got her clothes in a blaze, and was burned so as to produce death about nine o'clock on the following morning.

January 26, 1850

MARRIED

On the 20th inst., by the Rev. J. W. P. McKenzie, at the residence of Dr. G. H. Woolton, in this Town, Mr. Jas. W. Russell to Miss Susan A. Thomas.

February 16, 1850

DIED

At this town on the morning of the 20th ult., Alexander J. Russell, Esq., in the 30th year of his age, after an illnes of a little over three days. Mr. Russell left town on the afternoon of the 16th in the full enjoyment of excellent health, but during that night he was taken with a severe chill while encamped in the Sulphur bottom. Congestion of the brain especially set in, and from that time until his death he never spoke. He was brought home on the morning of Saturday, but to his afflicted wife, there was no look, no word of recognition, for the fell destroyer death had shot

THE NORTHERN STANDARD, CLARKSVILLE, TEXAS

his arrow with a too unerring aim. He lingered until the next morning.... A fond Wife and infant daughter have been deprived of their natural protector...

The Masonic fraternity, of which he was a worthy member, testified their estimation of the value in which they held him, by a large attendance on the day of his burial.

In this Town, on the 14th ult., of Consumption John C. Garrison, aged 26 years. Mr. Garrison was from Memphis, Tenn.

In this county, on the 30th ult., Susan Elizabeth, infant daughter of Wm. B. Stout, aged eleven months and twenty two days.

February 23, 1850

DIED

In this Town, on Monday evening last, Minerva Eliza, daughter of the Rev. John Anderson, aged 13 years.

March 2, 1850

SUICIDE

At Paris, Lamar County, John W. Hagee, by taking laudanum, on Wednesday.

September 21, 1850

MARRIED

On Wednesday, the 18th inst., by the Rev. Sam'l Corley, at Pee Dee, Lamar County, Dr. John McDonnal, of this place, to Miss Mary Ann Tinnin, daughter of Col. Wm. Tinnin.

October 26, 1850

MARRIED

At the residence of Mr. John Nunnellee, Sevier County, Ark., by Rev. Mr. Perkins, Mr. Ulysses H. Ware, formerly of this county, and late of Corsicana, Texas, to Miss Nancy Nunnellee, of Ark.

THE NORTHERN STANDARD, CLARKSVILLE, TEXAS

DIED

At the residence of Judge Mills, in this vicinity, on Tuesday last, Mr. Abner W. Thompson, of the Choctaw Nation, in the twenty third year of his age. The deceased was a Member of the order of Free and accepted Masons, and his corpse was attended to the grave, and interred by his brethren of this place.

January 4, 1851

MARRIED

At church, in San Marcos, on Sunday the 17th instant, by the Rev. Thomas A. Lancaster, Major Clement R. Johns, to Miss Amanda Durham, all of Hays county.

In Washington on the Brazos, on the 8th inst., by the Rev. Mr. Pierce, Hon. James S. Gillet, to Miss Elizabeth John, eldest daughter of Captain R. H. Harper of that place.

January 25, 1851

MARRIED

On the 3rd Dec., 1850, by the Rev. J. W. Whipple, Mr. Joseph Glover, to Miss Maria C. Johnson, both of Bastrop, Bastrop County, Texas.

February 8, 1851

MARRIED

At the residence of Dr. Hoxey, Washington County, on Tuesday, December 24th, 1850, by Rev. Mr. Peavee, Mr. Frank Hubert, to Miss Sarah Hoxey, daughter of Dr. Hoxey, all of this county.

February 15, 1851

OBITUARY

Died of consumption on the 16th October, 1850, at the residence of Captain Bundy, Van Zandt County, Texas, Rev. Samuel Foster Donnell. The subject of this notice early embraced religion, and attached himself to the Cumberland Presbyterian Church, he was always a consistent and devoted Member. He was sent by the Lebannon Presbytery, as a Missionary to Texas, where he faithfully labored for five or six years, until his death. His daily conduct, said to all, "Here is the way, walk you in it." It was remarked by Mr. Bundy that on the day of his death, he sang, and prayed, as well as he ever heard him, and said, "If this be death, it is nothing to die. Mark the perfect Man, Behold the upright; the end of that man is peace." Donnell died like a Christian.

By a resolution of the Synod of which Brother Donnell was a Member, in token of their high esteem. Jas. Sampson.

February 22, 1851

DIED

In Shreveport, on the 19th ult., after a severe illness, Capt. J. W. Gamble.

March 22, 1851

MARRIED

On the 9th inst., at the residence of her father in Sevier County, Ark., Paulina F., daughter of Wm. Bizzell, to Thos. D. Hudgins, Esq., of this place.

April 5, 1851

DIED

At Preston, Grayson County, Texas, of Nervous affection of the brain, John P. Reeves, late a resident of Hopkins County, aged 31 years. The deceased left four small children, and numerous friends, to mourn his loss, but their loss is His gain. G. P. R.

April 12, 1851

MARRIED

In this Town, on Thursday evening the 10th inst., by Hon. Hugh F. Young, Chief Justice of Red River County, Miss Annovanda Ribble, to Mr. John Cochran, all of this County.

April 19, 1851

DIED

In San Antonio on the 9th ult., Baron Armand Ducos de Montbrun, formerly an officer in the French service.

On the 31st Feb., [sic.] at his residence on the Lavaca, Maj. James Kerr, aged sixty years. He was a native of Kentucky, and emigrated to upper Louisiana before its transfer to the United States. He had been in many thrilling scenes of the frontier and Indian life in Missouri, filling various offices with marked distinction, and then removed to Texas

THE NORTHERN STANDARD, CLARKSVILLE, TEXAS

where he has been a resident for the last 26 years. He was one of Stephen F. Austin's particular friends. He held several offices of importance under the Mexican government. He also took a very active part in the Texian revolution: was a member of the Convention that declared the Independence of Texas, and was a member of Congress in 1838-39.

June 7, 1851

DIED

At his residence in this County, on Wednesday morning last, of disease of the kidneys, Dr. Martin Guest, an old respected citizen.

At the residence of John Montgomery, Esq., in this town, on Wednesday evening, of disease of the brain, Cina, daughter of B. H. and Amanda Epperson, aged 16 months.

August 16, 1851

OBITUARY NOTICE

Died, by drowning on Sunday the 10th inst., Mr. Thomas C. Burks, aged 19 years, five months and eighteen days. Son of Joseph H. Burks, Esq., of Bowie County.
The deceased has resided in Clarksville for more than a year, where he was engaged in the study of Medicine under Dr. A. K. Elliott.

October 4, 1851

MARRIED

On the 30th of September, 1851, by the Rev. Samuel Corley, Mr. W. L. Nunneley of Sevier County, Ark., to Miss Nancy A. Ware, of Red River Co., Texas.

FIRE IN CLARKSVILLE

We have this week, to record the first serious Conflagration, which has ever taken place in our town. On Friday morning last about two o'clock, the citizens were awakened by an alarm of fire, and attracted by the light, proceeded to the public square, and found the large building known as the Star Hotel, on fire, and making a most brilliant illumination. The air was still, hardly a perceptible current, and to that only are we indebted, that there is a house left around the square. All of them are of wood, highly combustible. The hotel was only occupied at one end room, by Trimble and Hudgins, as a law office, and was soon consumed, most of their books and papers being destroyed, from the fact,

THE NORTHERN STANDARD, CLARKSVILLE, TEXAS

that so unusual is an alarm of fire in our quiet village, and so little the preparation for indicating it, that until the hotel was fully enveloped in fire, but few were present, and they were looking out for houses that were filled with merchandise or furniture.

From the hotel the fire communicated itself to the opposite store occupied by Wm. P. Dickson, with a Masonic lodge above, and thence spreading easterly and northerly, it destroyed the law offices of Mills & Murray, and A. Morrill, the confectionary of Geo. Fiedson, the tailor shop of Wm. Crittendon, and the house occupied by Dr. Geo. Gordon as an office, and Tho's R. Wilson as a saddler's shop. The fine residence of Dr. Boyce at one end, and the hotel of Mrs. Caton at the other, were saved by wet blankets and carpets. The grocery store of J. C. Hart was saved in the same way. As we said before, had there been a breath of air the square would have been swept.

The town has no such possessions as a fire engine. All the contents of store, offices and shops, except the office of Trimble and Hudgins were removed. During the progress of the flames an ineffectual attempt to blow up a house with powder was made, and failed from a want of knowledge of the true manner of doing it. The buildings were most of them small, and the actual loss does not exceed seven thousand dollars.

The fire was quite an event in our village life, and doubtless will induce the purchase of several of Philip's fire annihilators, as soon as they can be procured. It originated in the kitchen back of the Star Hotel, where some persons are said to have been amusing themselves with a small game of cards. Whether the grand jury will consider the results of sufficient importance to warrant an enquiry by them into the particulars of the game aforesaid, remains to be seen.

December 6, 1851

MARRIED

On Thursday night last, at the residence of Geo. H. Bagby, Esq., near Clarksville, by the Rev. Jas. Guthrie, Mr. James W. Russell and Miss Lucy Jane Bagby.

DIED

In Bowie County, Texas, on Monday the 17th day of November 1851, Mary Elizabeth Birdwell, consort of Elijah M. Birdwell, aged 47 years, 8 months.

December 20, 1851

DIED

At the residence of James C. Caldwell, on Friday

THE NORTHERN STANDARD, CLARKSVILLE, TEXAS

morning the 19th inst., Oliver Ramsdall, in the 68 year of his age.

December 25, 1851

MARRIED

In Galveston, on the evening of the 30th ult., by the Rev. Mr. Eaton, Gen. T. J. Chambers to Miss Abby Chubb.

January 3, 1852

DIED

At his residence adjoining the town, on the 30th of December, Dr. Thomas D. Lee, aged 40 years, 5 months and 3 days.   (Philadelphia papers please copy.)

January 10, 1852

DIED

In California, on the 21st August, Mrs. Sarah Wooldridge, wife of Mr. John R. Wooldridge, formerly of Austin, Texas, aged 24 years.

January 24, 1852

MARRIED

At the residence of Mr. John C. Carter, adjoining this town, by the Hon. Wm. S. Todd, on the 8th inst., Miss Catherine Gaines and Mr. James B. Snelser, both of this vicinage.

DIED

Near Sonora, California, Nov. 3rd, 1851, of cronic diarrhea, Thomas L. Vining, son of Wade H. Vining, Esq., of this County, aged 24 years and 8 months.

February 7, 1852

DIED

At Corsicana, Navarro County, on the 22nd ult., of Pneumonia, Dr. Joel A. Wooten, formerly of this County, and originally from Wilks County, Georgia, aged 29 years.

THE NORTHERN STANDARD, CLARKSVILLE, TEXAS

February 28, 1852

MARRIED

On Sunday the 13th inst., by the Rev. Mr. Pevey, Miss Cornellia Clark, to Mr. A. N. Witherspoon, late Editor and Proprietor of the Star State Patriot.

July 10, 1852

OBITUARY

Mrs. Smithey Jane Runnels, consort of Howell R. Runnels, Esq., of Bowie County, Texas, was removed to the saint's everlasting rest, on Sunday 13th inst., in the 25 year of her age.

July 17, 1852

MARRIED

On the 27th of April, by the Rev. R. R. Tucker, C. E. F. Boyer, Esq., to Miss Sarah E. Pegues, all of Collin County, Texas.

September 11, 1852

MARRIED

On Tuesday morning, August 24th, in Cass Co., Texas, by the Rev. H. B. Dye, Sam F. Mosely, Esq., of Jefferson, to Miss Eliza G., daughter of Seaborn J. Wilkinson, of Caddo Parish, Louisiana.

September 18, 1852

DIED

Of congestive fever, in Paradise, Cass county, Texas, on the 27th August, Mrs. Barbara Braiolic Rogers, consort of Gen. James Harrison Rogers.

October 2, 1852

MARRIED

On Thursday night last, by the Rev. Sam Corley, Mr. William M. Thomas, to Miss Margaret D. Foreman, daughter of Wm. W. Foreman, all of this County.

THE NORTHERN STANDARD, CLARKSVILLE, TEXAS

October 5 [sic] 1852

DIED

In Clarksville on the 15th of September, Mr. B. F. Harris, of Lynchburg, Va., in the 27th year of his age. (Lynchburg [Va.] Papers, please copy.)

November 20, 1852

MARRIED

At the residence of Josiah Davidson, near Town, by the Rev. J. W. P. McKenzie, Mr. Milton J. Mullins, to Miss Mary Davidson.

December 18, 1852

DIED

In Jefferson, on the 17th inst., Mr. Henry Gooding, in the 40th year of his age.

January 8, 1853

DIED

At his residence, near Clarksville, on Friday night the 7th inst., of Pneumonia, Wm. Trimble, Esq., aged 54 years.
The deceased was formerly a Judge of the Federal Court for the Territory of Arkansas, but had lived in this State for the last five years...

MARRIED

On Thursday evening, by the Rev. W. M. Pickett, Mr. Calvin Dale, to Miss Sarah West, daughter of Cap. John W. West, all of this county.

January 22, 1853

DIED

On the 19th of December last, at her residence in Sabine Town, in Sabine County, Mrs. Jane R. Kaufman, widow of the late Hon. David S. Kaufman. Mrs. Kaufman died of a disease of the lungs under which she had suffered for several years.

At their residence near Clarksville, on the 18th inst., Maria Louise, the youngest daughter of L. R. and E. M. Henderson aged 10 months and 16 days.

THE NORTHERN STANDARD, CLARKSVILLE, TEXAS

January 29, 1853

OBITUARY

Died in this town, on the morning of the 21st inst., in her 40th year, at the house of her son-in-law, J. A. N. Murray, Esq., Mrs. Susan M. James, wife of Col. L. M. James, formerly of Marshall Co., North Miss.

February 5, 1853

MARRIED

At the residence of Col. E. Nelms, near Anderson, Grimes county, Hon. John H. Reagan, to Miss Edwina A. Nelms.

February 12, 1853

DIED

In Paris, Lamar County, Texas, on the 13th of January, 1853, Ester Annie Davidson, Consort of Hopkins Davidson of that place, and Daughter of Capt. David Doak, of Red River County, aged 35 years, 4 months and 5 days. She left a fond husband and five children.

March 5, 1853

MARRIED

In Louisville, Arkansas, on Thursday evening 17th last, by James J. Battle, Esq., Miss Jane M., daughter of Bolin Stricklin, dec'd., to Mr. Julian D. Battle of Myrtle Springs, Texas.

OBITUARY

Died in Dallas, on the 25th January, 1853, in the 29th year of her age, Mrs. Elizabeth Ann McPherson ... She leaves a husband and five children to bemourn her loss. (Fort Smith and Van Buren papers will please copy.)

March 12, 1853

DIED

On the 1st of March, in the 26th year of her age, Mrs. Emma Morgan, consort of Mr. S. H. Morgan, of Clarksville, and 2nd daughter of Mr. Josiah and Frances Garland, of Lewisville, Arkansas.

THE STANDARD, CLARKSVILLE, TEXAS

April 9, 1853

AWFUL MURDER

It is our painful duty to state that our county man Mr. Gaffeene who was found dead near his own house, on the road a few weeks since, and who was supposed to have been killed by a kick from his horse--was basely murdered by two of his own negroes, who are now in jail at this place. They have not only confessed the fact of the murder, but they have made a full disclosure of all the particluars. They have produced the club with which they knocked him off his horse and murdered him.

May 14, 1853

OBITUARY

Died, in Clarksville, Texas, after a brief illness, Mr. Wm. Hatten Thomson, formerly of Union District, South Carolina, aged 49 years, 9 months, 10 days. [Lengthy eulogy follows.]

NOTICE

Gen. T. J. Rusk, of Texas, has left Washington for New York to infuse life, it is said, into the Pacific Railroad Company, now forming in that city. He is entirely sanguine of the early commencement and rapid completion of that immense enterprise.

May 21, 1853

MARRIED

On the 1st of May, at the residence of Jas. C. Caldwell, near town, by the Rev. Sam'l Corley, Dr. John B. Harris to Miss Martha Ann Caldwell.

At Waxahatchie, on the 1st May, by the Rev'd James Loyd, Dr. Wm. T. Briggs, to Miss Mary Catharine Rogers, daughter of E. C. Rogers, Esq.

In this place, on the 17th inst., by the Rev. Samuel Corley, Dr. D. H. Gibson to Miss Lizzie F., daughter of the late John Gattis, Esq. [N.B.-- Romney and Abingdon, Virginia, papers will please copy.]

June 4, 1853

FOUND GUILTY

The Negro slaves John and Mose, the property of the late William Gaffeney, were this morning placed upon trial, charged with the murder of their master William Gaffeney, on the 21st of March last. They pled not guilty. [More follows.]

June 11, 1853

MARRIED

At the residence of Mr. Laboon on Pine Creek, on the 26th ult., by W. Fleming, Esq., Mr. James Coffman to Miss Rachael Laboon, all of this county.

On Sunday the 22nd April, by the Rev'd John Myers, Mr. A. Fyke to Miss Jemina Myers, all of Dallas County, Texas.

DIED

On the 14th of April, 1853, on board the steam boat Preston on his way to Virginia, in the 56th year of his age, Timothy Wortham of Red River County, Texas. The deceased was a native of Virginia, and had been a resident of Texas, about 5 years preceding his death. [More follows.]

June 18, 1853

MARRIED

At the residence of Capt. John A. Bagby, in this town, on Sunday morning last, by the Rev. J. W. P. McKenzie, Dr. P. W. Birmingham of Fannin County, to Mrs. Mary Ann Haynes.

OBITUARY

Mrs. Winnifred B. Burks, consort of Col. Joseph H. Burks, departed this life at their residence in this town, on the 28th ult., in the forty fifth year of her age.
Our friend, of whom this hasty sketch is but a feeble memorial, was born in the County of Wilks, State of Georgia, whence with her husband she imigrated to Texas in 1846... [More follows.]

June 25, 1853

OBITUARY

Departed this life on Friday the 20th inst., in this

THE STANDARD, CLARKSVILLE, TEXAS

place, Mrs. Elizabeth Ward, mother of Dr. William, and Col. Mat Ward. [More follows.]

MARRIED

On Sunday evening the 29th ult. at Crockett, by James Bracken, Esq. the Hon. John E. Cravens, of this place, to Miss Mary B. Alford, of Crockett. [Trinity Advocate.]

August 6, 1853

OBITUARY

AT A REGULAR MEETING OF WILDEY LODGE, NO. 21
I. O. O. F. PARIS, TEXAS, JULY 26, 1853.
The death of Brother S. G. Swan being announced, the undersigned were appointed a Committee to draft resolutions expressive of the deep sorrow felt by the members of this Lodge, on being informed of the death of S. G. Swan, our former D.D. G. M. which occurred at Henderson, on the 5th of this inst.

August 13, 1853

MARRIED

In this town, on Wednesday evening last, by the Rev. Sam Corley, Mr. Charles Dillahunty to Miss Frances Norwood.

MURDER

Yesterday morning, our fellow citizen Mr. John Wilkins, of the firm of Epperson and Wilkins, was murdered in the blacksmith shop attached to the steam saw Mill, about ten miles north of Town, by a Negro named Washington, the property of Mr. E.

August 27, 1853

MARRIED

On Wednesday the 10th August by Rev. Mr. Hughes, Mr. Lafayette Smith to Miss Margaret Daniels, both of the County of Dallas, Texas.

September 3, 1853

DIED

On Wednesday, the 27th July, at his residence at Rugglesville, Choctaw Nation, near Fort Washita, Charles A. Galloway, Esq., in the 35 year of his age.

THE STANDARD, CLARKSVILLE, TEXAS

On the 27th of July, at Hubbardston, Mass., after a severe and protracted illness, Lucy, wife of J. H. Heald, Esq., New Orleans.

September 24, 1853

DIED

In Austin, on the 8th of August, Mr. William Lawrence, formerly of Red River County, Texas, a most worthy and estimable citizen.

October 22, 1853

MARRIED

On the 28 ultimo, at Brooklyn, by the Rev. Dr. Bethune, Colonel Morgan L. Smith, formerly of N.Y. City, but now of Columbia, Texas, to Miss Elizabeth B. Brower, daughter of Captain John H. Brower.

November 19, 1853

DIED

At James Elliot's, near Unionville, Texas, on Saturday night the 29th of October, Felix Morse, apparently about 40 years of age. The deceased was from Gordon County [Georgia?]

December 31, 1853

MARRIED

In Lamar County, December 21st, 1853, at the residence of James S. Bridge, by Dr. Padon, of the Church of God, Mr. James Stephenson and Miss Katherine W. Bridge, daughter of the above.

DIED

At her plantation, in Jefferson County, Arkansas, on the 11th inst., at 6 o'clock p.m., of pleurisy, Mrs. Catharine H. Washington, aged 45 years.

January 21, 1854

MARRIED

At McKinney, Collin County, on the 10th inst., Dr. H. C. Haynes to Miss Margaret Hart.

DIED

At the residence of his father, of congestive chill, on Thursday last, Wm. W. Duty, aged about 23 years.

February 11, 1854

MARRIED

At the residence of Mr. Joseph Williams, near town, on Wednesday evening last, by the Rev. Sam Corley, Dr. James M. Norwood, to Miss Ann E. Williams.

DIED

In this town on Sunday morning the 29th Mrs. Sarah Mitchell aged 60 years, a native of Virginia near Richmond, and subsequently a resident of Alabama. The deceased had resided here for fourteen years.

February 18, 1854

MARRIED

In Dallas County on Wednesday the 18th ultimo, at the residence of O. W. Knight, by the Rev. James A. Smith, Nat M. Burford, Esq., to Miss Mary J. Knight, all of that county.

March 11, 1854

DIED

At his residence near DeKalb, Bowie County, Sunday night last, Allen H. Collom.

May 6, 1854

MARRIED

On the 25th inst., by the Rev. John ..., Mr. John L. Lovejoy, Jr. of McKinney to Miss Nancy Douglass of Collin County.

May 27, 1854

DIED

Died of Billious Intermittant Fever, on the morning of Thursday, the 11 inst., at the residence of James C. Caldwell, of this county in the 15th year of her age, Anna Mercer, oldest daughter of the late James H. Johnson...

June 3, 1854

OBITUARY

Departed this life on the morning of the 2nd June 1854, at his residence in Red River County, Capt. Wade Hampton Vining. The mournful event was sudden and unlooked for by his family and friends. Being sick not more than one week he suffered a great deal from the violence of the disease, but died, as he had lived with perfect calmness and resignation. Capt. Vining was born on the 26th day of April 1793, in Anson County, North Carolina, but removed with his father and family, in the year 1810, to Limestone County, in the State of Alabama, where he continued to reside, performing all the duties of a good citizen, until the fall of 1835, when he emigrated to this country, and settled at his late residence, at that time in the State of Coahuila and Texas.

Ever ready to respond to the call of duty, he served his native country in the celebrated Creek war, and participated in the fearful struggles of his adopted land, in the days of her infancy and weakness. As the best evidence of the purity of his character, and the integrity of his principles, he received repeated evidence of the public confidence, in every place he lived. He served for a long time as Sheriff of Limestone County, Alabama, and filled the responsible station of Clerk of the District Court of Red River County, from the organization of the County until August 1850...

June 10, 1854

MARRIED

At Fort Washita, C.N., on the 16th ult., by Rev. E. Couch, Mr. Richard T. Cobb, merchant of Woodboro, Grayson County, Texas, to Miss Mary Ellen, eldest daughter of Lemuel Gooding, Esq., of Fort Washita.

In Nacogdoches, at the residence of the bride's father, on the 18th inst., Gen. J. H. Rogers, of Jefferson, to Miss C. A. Ochiltree, eldest daughter of Hon. W. B. Ochiltree.

July 8, 1854

DIED

In this town on Sunday evening last, suddenly, Mr. Charles H. Peabody, formerly of Nashville, Tenn., aged 27 years.

In this town on Wednesday morning last, of Congestion, Mrs. Margaret Bagby, wife of Geo. H. Bagby, daughter of James Latimer, Esq., aged 40 years.

July 22, 1854

DIED

Alexander M. Crooks, Esq., for several years a Justice of the Peace for this precinct, and for several years in failing health from a Pulmonary affection, was attacked by a hemorrhage of the lungs, on his way from his office to his residence, yesterday about mid-day, and died at the house of Mr. Stephen, in a few minutes after reaching it; being unable to get home. Mr. Crooks was an intelligent and in all respects a good citizen, and had filled his official position most acceptably for a long time. He leaves a large family to mourn his loss.

August 12, 1854

DIED

At Myrtle Springs, on Sunday July 1st, of Acute Gastritis, Diana C., wife of James W. Battle, and the daughter of Josiah W. and Diana C. Fort. She was born November 11th, 1833, was married January 22, 1852. She leaves a husband and a little daughter.

August 19, 1854

MARRIED

Near Warren, on the 9th instant, by Rev. Dr. Walker, Mr. J. R. Russell, Merchant of Bonham, to Miss Cynthia Bradford, daughter of J. F. Bradford, Esq.

DIED

On the 16th ult., of a Congestive Chill, in the 51st year of her age, Mrs. Jane, consort of Nelson Doak, Esq., of this place.

August 26, 1854

DIED

In this town, on Tuesday last, the 22nd inst., of Bronchitis, Mrs. Eliza A. Todd, consort of Wm. S. Todd, and daughter of Col. Thomas Hudgins, formerly of Mathews County, Virginia, aged 40 years, 7 months and 8 days...
    Mrs. Todd came to Texas in 1844, and during most of the intervening period has been the Teacher of a Female Institute...

September 9, 1854

MARRIED

On the evening of the 7th instant, by Rev. S. P. Corley, Mr. Wm. N. Crosby, of South Carolina, and Miss Mary Jane Lee, of this place.

DIED

In Austin on the 29th inst., Captain H. G. Catlett, aged about 40 years.

September 23, 1854

MARRIED

At the residence of Mrs. Beatie in Red River County on Thursday the 14th inst., by the Rev. Mr. Corley, Mr. James M. Murphy, of Jefferson, to Miss Martha Hamblin.

September 30, 1854

MURDER

On Wenesday at about eleven o'clock, Samuel Sinclair was killed, at Pine Bluff in this County, while standing in the door of his Grocery. No one was seen to perpetrate the offence, but Lovett Cady living oposite was arrested upon suspicion, and after examination before P. H. Fleming, J.P., was bound over to appear at the next term of the District Court for this County.

October 7, 1854

MARRIED

In Titus County, on the 21st ult., by Malcolm Bolin, Esq., Mr. Robert Hays to Miss Rebecca Keener.

October 21, 1854

MARRIED

On the 28th ult., by the Rev. J. F. Ford, Dr. J. H. Lewis of Shreveport, to Miss Ada S. Todd, daughter of James D. Todd, Esq., of Smithland, Texas.

OBITUARY

Died on the 6th inst., at her father's, Lemuel

THE STANDARD, CLARKSVILLE, TEXAS

Gooding, Esq., Fort Washita, Mrs. Mary Ellen Cobb, wife of Mr. R. T. Cobb, Merchant of Woodboro, Texas, after an illness of four days.

November 11, 1854

Mortuary

Departed this life at the residence of his brother, George Ury, two miles from Jefferson, on the 26 of October 1854, at 25 minutes before 7 o'clock A.M., Amos Ury in the 49th year of his age. He was born in the State of Tennessee in the year 1806 and emigrated to Texas in 1835, then a wilderness with but few settlers, and attended with hardships and privations which men of nerve and worth alone could overcome. After several years successful struggle with the adversities of a new country, and having by great industry and economy acquired considerable property and a vast credit, he removed and settled in the town of Jefferson. He was among its earliest citizens, and here as a merchant he laid the foundation of his handsome fortune... He leaves a wife and four children...

November 25, 1854

MARRIED

On Thursday evening the 16th inst., at the residence of the Hon. E. Cross, of Hempstead Co., Ark., by the Rev. J. R. Annis, J. L. Witherspoon, Esq., of Arkadelphia, to Miss Mary Frances, daughter of the Hon. Edward Cross, of that county.

December 2, 1854

OBITUARY

Departed this life in DeKalb, Bowie Co., Texas, on Saturday 25th November, of pneumonia, Sarah M., the only child of Dr. Martin, late dec'd., and Lucy N. Cornelius, aged 20 months.

December 16, 1854

DIED

In Tarrant, Hopkins County, of typhoid fever, on the 7th inst., Dr. B. S. Bailey, aged 26 years.

December 23, 1854

MARRIED

On Wednesday evening last, at the residence of Col. L. D. Henderson, near town, by the Rev. J. W. P. McKenzie, Mr....Tuttle, of Sherman, to Miss Virginia Henderson.

January 27, 1855

DIED

Departed this life, the 14th inst., in the vicinity of Bowie County, in the 52nd year of his age, Dr. James Read, late of Alabama, but for the last twelve months a resident of Bowie County...Dr. Read leaves an interesting family, a wife and six children who have the deep sympathy of their acquaintances.

In Washington, Arkansas, the 7th inst., James P. Jett, in the 47th year of his age.

February 3, 1855

DIED

At the residence of her father, in Mount Pleasant, Titus County, Texas, on the 22nd day of January 1855, under most distressing circumstances, Anna M. L. Hendricks, aged four years and nine months, daughter of Dr. John and Mary F. Hendricks. [More follows.]

February 24, 1855

DIED

In New Orleans, on the 5th inst., Capt. Benjamin Crooks, aged 56 years. Captain Crooks being one of the oldest steamboat captains on the western waters, all the steamboats in port hung their flags at half mast.

March 3, 1855

DIED

At the residence of Dr. Meaux, in Amelia County, Va., on the evening of the 16th inst., Miss Lucy G. Gaines, younger daughter of Robert H. [E.?] Gaines.

THE STANDARD, CLARKSVILLE, TEXAS

March 10, 1855

OBITUARY

Died at his residence in Boston, Texas, on the 3rd of March, William C. Daniel, aged about 35 years.
Mr. Daniel was a native of Tennessee but had been a citizen of Bowie County for the last twelve years.

March 24, 1855

DIED

Of pneumonia at the residence of Mr. F. Dawson, in Hot Springs Co., Ark., Samuel Carmack, of Williamson Co., Texas, on the 27th day of February, 1855, aged 60 years. It is not known where the relations of the deceased reside. [Texas and Louisiana papers will confer a favor by copying.]

April 7, 1855

MARRIED

On Sunday the first day of April, by the Rev. John M. Waskum, Frank H. Clark, Esq., of Jefferson, to Miss Annie R. Hawkins, of Cass Co.

April 14, 1855

DIED

In Boston [Bowie Co.] on the 21st ultimo, George, eldest son of Mrs. Julia Love, in the 28th year of his age...

Among the many who have fallen victims to the late and yet lingering epidemic, is numbered Mrs. Catharine Maulding, who departed this life the 18th inst., in the 53rd year of her age, relict of the late Mr. Presley Maulding, one of the early settlers of Bowie County...

April 28, 1855

DIED

In this place, of consumption, at the residence of his mother, at 2 o'clock a.m., on 25th inst., Mr. George W. Slayton, in the 26th year of his age.

THE STANDARD, CLARKSVILLE, TEXAS

May 26, 1855

MARRIED

In Collin County on the 6th inst., at the residence of Maj. Sam Bogart, J. H. Harbenger, Esq., of McKinney, to Miss Margaret Ellen Bogart. [Louisville, Ky., papers please copy.]

DIED

On Monday last, 21st instant, of hemorrhage of the lungs, Mr. D. G. Dill, of this place, formerly editor of the Choctaw Telegraph, published at Doaksville, C.N.

June 9, 1855

DIED

At his residence, near town, on Friday night of last week, of consumption, Wm. T. Montgomery, aged 45 years, 6 months and 12 days, formerly of Giles Co., Tennessee...
The bereaved partner and four little children he has left behind, will mourn for many a day...

August 4, 1855

DIED

At her residence near Oak Hill, Lafayette County, Ark., on the 3rd ult., of pleurisy, in the 42nd year of her age, Mrs. Sarah Catherine, wife of R. B. Duty.

MARRIED

In this town, on Tuesday the 31st, by the Rev. John Anderson, Dr. Eugene B. Rochelle, of Bowie County, to Miss Catherine S. Anderson, daughter of the officiating clergyman.

November 17, 1855

OBITUARY

Died on the 19th of October, 1855, at her residence in DeKalb, Texas, Mary G. Smith, in the 76th year of her age. She was a native of North Carolina, and has resided at different periods in Tennessee, Alabama and Mississippi. She leaves a large circle of friends and relatives to mourn her loss...

THE STANDARD, CLARKSVILLE, TEXAS

November 24, 1855

DIED

On the 22nd inst., in this place, Mrs. Mary Montgomery, consort of Mr. John Montgomery, in her seventy-eighth year.

December 1, 1855

DIED

In Anderson, Grimes County, Texas, on the 15th November, Lewis D. Baker, formerly a respected resident of this county, and previously from Lebanon, Tennessee, aged 41 years.

December 15, 1855

DIED

At the place of Col. Joseph H. Burks, near town, on Saturday morning, last, of pneumonia, Frank Thomson, formerly a resident of Bowie and Red River Counties...late of Wharton County.

January 26, 1856

OBITUARY

Died, on the Monday of the 17th instant after a few days illness, at the residence of her parents, aged ten years and two days, Eliza, third daughter of Ezekiel and Sally Wallis.

May 3, 1856

DIED

Departed this life at Black Hawk, Carrol County, Miss., in the full hope of a blissful immortality, Mrs. Sharkey, consort of Mr. Greenwood L. Sharkey and eldest daughter of Mr. J. J. Williams of Boston, Bowie County... A little mound near the banks of the Yazoo River, contains all of her that could die...

May 10, 1856

DIED

John A. Bagby, Esq., aged 66 years and seven months,

at his residence in Clarksville, Texas, on the 4th inst., after a protracted illness, disease of the heart, which he bore with much submission, and when the king of terrors arrived, he met him with much resignation.

May 24, 1856

MARRIED

On the 7th of April, at Clarksville by the Rev. A. L. Davis, Alfred T. Howard, Esq., to Miss Sallie R. Dickson, daughter of Maj. Jno. B. Dickson.

RESOLUTION

At a regular communication of Boston Lodge No. 69, the following Preamble and Resolutions were adopted.
Whereas - It has pleased our all wise Parent to remove from our midst our worthy and well Beloved Brother, J. C. Barber....

May 31, 1856

OBITUARY

The Nacogdoches Chronicle announces the death of Mrs. Rusk:
"She died at her residence near Nacogdoches, at two o'clock on the morning of the 26th inst., aged forty-six years, eight months and twelve days.
Mrs. Rusk was born in 1806, in Habersham County, Georgia, and was a daughter of the Hon. Benjamin Cleveland, of that state. In 1827 married our present distinguished Senator, Thomas J. Rusk, then a young and rising lawyer of that state."

June 7, 1856

MARRIED

On the 15th day of May, 1856, by Rev. Thos. F. Garrison, Mr. Chas. J. Anderson of Kentucky to Miss Sarah A. Russell, of Sherman, Grayson County, Texas.

At the residence of Thomas Willison, Esq., Hopkins County, on 2nd ult., by Josiah Smith, Esq., Mr. Hugh M. Stewart of Titus Co., to Mary Ann Willison.

DIED

In Grayson County, on the 6th day of May, A.D. 1856, Celestia Virginia Adsette Bone, daughter of John W. Bone and Elizabeth A. Bone, aged four years, ten months, and four days.

THE STANDARD, CLARKSVILLE, TEXAS

June 21, 1856

NOTICE

Gen. Rusk is still at home. He has had a severe attack of illness since his return, which together with the effect of the sad bereavement he has experienced, will prevent his early return to Washington. At one time his life was despaired of, but we are happy to say that he is now convalescent.   Nacogdoches Chronicle, June 3rd.

July 12, 1856

MARRIED

In Boston, Bowie County, at the residence of Wm. B. Featherston, Esq., on the evening of the 20th ult., by the Rev. Jesse A. Witt, Mr. John W. Doty [Duty?] to Miss Martha E. Featherston.

August 2, 1856

OBITUARY

Dr. Lemuel Peters is no more. Though in the prime of manhood, he has been cut off by the ruthless hand of death. He died at his residence in Boston, Bowie County, Texas, on the 6th day of June, in the 37th year of his age... He was for several years, a consistent and worthy member of the Baptist Church. Let his bereaved wife and dear little ones, whom he left, take consolation to themselves, that their husband and father is not dead but sleepeth.

Died at Paris, Texas, on the morning of the 8th of July, James S., infant son of Lewis S. and Annie V. Wells, aged eight months and nine days. [Philadelphia North American, and Saturday Evening Post please copy.]

August 23, 1856

MARRIED

By Chief Justice Harman, of Hopkins Co., at the residence of Wm. Strother, Mr. John M. Ewing to Miss Sarah E. Strother, all of that county.

September 6, 1856

DIED

On Friday morning of sporadic dysentery, Miss Margaret S. Doak, aged 18 years, daughter of Nelson Doak, Esq.

THE TEXAS REPUBLICAN, MARSHALL, TEXAS

June 15, 1849

FUNERAL

The funeral sermon of Rev. H. B. Kelsey, will be preached at this place, on Sunday, the 24th inst., by the Rev. S. W. Williams.

AWFUL AFFAIR

We learn by a citizen of Cherokee County, that Col. Hogg killed Rufus Chandler, shooting him with a double-barrel shot gun and two pistols. Mr. C. is said to have been shockingly mangled- both were citizens of Rusk in Cherokee County. We are not sufficiently informed of the circumstances that led to this fatal deed, to attempt to give them. The affair took place on Sunday last, 10th inst.

August 3, 1849

MARRIED

On the 26th ult., in this place, by the Rev. N. W. Burks, Maj. Ed. Clark, to Miss Martha Evans, daughter of Dr. Evans, all of this place.

With the above, we received a choice piece of wedding cake.

August 23, 1849

DIED

On the evening of the 10th inst., at his residence in Dr. Field's neighborhood, in this county, Mr. R. S. Hightower. His attack was sudden, and the nature of it not known.
"The good man's fate is privileged beyond the walks
Of virtuous life, quite in the verge of heaven."

Departed this life, at his residence, about ten miles from this place, on the 15th instant, at 7 o'clock, P.M., John P. Thompson, in the 46th year of his age, after about eight months affliction, which he bore with great patience and resignation. His disease was consumption.

The deceased was born in Washington County, Ala., and descended from a highly respectable family. He removed to the state of Mississippi some fifteen or twenty years ago, where he resided until about eighteen months past, when he removed to Caddo Parish, La., and from thence to this county.
[Lengthy eulogy follows.]

THE TEXAS REPUBLICAN, MARSHALL, TEXAS

September 6, 1849

OBITUARY

Departed this life, on the 2d inst., between the hours of 6 and 7 o'clock, A.M., at his residence, in this county, Charles Livingston, in the 39th year of his age.
The deceased was a native of the State of North Carolina. He emigrated from the State of Alabama, about the year 1840, to this county, where he continued to reside till his death.
He was a prominent member of the Methodist Church. He was unsullied in his character, exemplary in his life, and triumphant in his death. He has exchanged this world, with all its goods and ills, its joys and griefs, for his reward in the Kingdom of his Redeemer. The wife of his bosom has lost a tender and loving companion, and society a worthy member- but their loss, is His eternal gain.

September 27, 1849

OBITUARY

Departed this life, on the 25th inst., Mrs. Sarah D. Gregg, consort of G. G. Gregg, of this place, in the 23d year of her age.
The deceased was an amiable member of society. She has left an affectionate husband and two small children, besides numerous relatives and friends, to mourn her loss.

October 4, 1849

OBITUARY

A sad breach, not soon to be repaired, has recently been made in the circles of our town, both family, social, and religious, in the death of Mrs. Sarah D. Gregg, wife of Mr. George G. Gregg, and daughter of Dr. Wm. Evans.
Mrs. Gregg was born on the 18th March, 1827, and died on the 27th September, 1849, being in her 23d year.
She made a profession of faith in the Redeemer, and was baptized by Elder John Bryce, in November, 1848, and united with the Baptist Church at Marshall; in the fellowship of which, she pursued a course of active, but unobtrusive piety, till her last moment...   [Lengthy eulogy follows.]

October 11, 1849

OBITUARY

Departed this life, on the morning of the 10th inst., Mrs. Frances Harris, consort of Mr. Micajah Harris, of this place.

We are not advised of the age of the deceased, though she was considerably advanced on the downward journey of life. She had for many years been a truly pious member of the Methodist Episcopal Church, and had an assurance to the last that her hope was not in vain.

October 25, 1849

OBITUARY

Departed this life, at Carthage, in the 15th year of her age, on the evening of the 13th inst., Miss Martha McCary, daughter of Mr. N. D. and Mrs. C. McCary.

The deceased had been a member of the Methodist Episcopal Church for several years previous to her death, in which she manifested a lively hope of her acceptance with the Redeemer.

December 6, 1849

MARRIED

On the evening of the 29th ult., by the Rev. Wm. Steel, Mr. F. M. Campbell, to Mrs. E. A. Russell, both of this county.

We received a choice piece of the wedding-cake with the above notice. As upon all such occasions, we wish the happy pair a life of felicity.

On the 29th ult., by T. A. Harris, Esq., Sydney B. Goodwin, to Miss Minerva A. Stroud, both of this place.

On the 29th ult., by T. A. Harris, Esq., John Williams, to Iraanna W. Stroud, both of this place.

January 10, 1850

OBITUARY

Departed this life, at his residence, in Panola Co., Texas, on the 24th Oct., 1849, in the 70th year of his age, Abner Herrin, Esq., the patriarch of a respectful family. [Lengthy eulogy follows.]

April 11, 1850

OBITUARY

Marshall Lodge, No.22, April 6, 1850.
"Heaven from all creatures hides the book of fate,
All but the page preceived."

Pope.

W. B. Patton, aged 23 years, departed this life on the 13th ult. He had been a member of this lodge about eight months preceding his death. As citizen he was generally respected; as a Mason, he was zealous, and beloved. [Masonic resolution follows.]

July 6, 1850

MARRIED

On the 2d instant by the Rev. R. T. Mitchell, Maxfield Anderson, Esq., to Miss A. E. J. Hall, all of this county.

On the evening of the 4th of July, at the Baptist Church, by the Rev. A. H. Shanks, Rev. F. H. Blades to Miss Julia A. Taylor, daughter of Jos. M. Taylor of this place.

In Mobile, Ala., on the 30th ult., by the Rev. J. Hutchinson, Mr. Uriam T. Kenan, of Dallas County, to Miss Elizabeth Louisiana Holcombe, daughter of H. B. Holcombe, Esq.

DIED

In this place, on the 25th of June, 1850, very suddenly, of apoplexy, Mr. Samuel Burton, late of Birmingham, England.

On the 27th of June, Sarah Ann, daughter of the above, of fever.

August 10, 1850

OBITUARY

Departed this life at her residence in this county on the 23d of July, Mrs. Carolina Hunter, consort of B. B. B. Hunter, in the 30th year of her age, after a protracted sickness of several weeks, which she bore with remarkable fortitude and unfaltering patience. In the various relations of life-as wife, mother, and mistress-she was truly exemplary and worthy of all imitation. Of a warm and social disposition, she delighted to cultivate her acquaintance with her neighbors, and to render all as happy and as agreeable as possible, within the sphere of her intercourse.
She has left a devoted husband and five children to mourn their irreparable bereavement. May He, who "tempers the wind to the shorn lamb," throw around them, in an especial manner, the mantle of his everlasting protection; and when with them life's busy dream is o'er, may they be re-united in the paradise of God, where sorrows and sighing flee away, and where they will be forever more at rest.   M.

THE TEXAS REPUBLICAN, MARSHALL, TEXAS

August 24, 1850

DIED

In this place, on the morning of the 13th instant, about 1 o'clock, A.M., at the residence of his brother, T. A. Harris, after a short illness, J. C. Harris, in the 22d year of his age.

September 7, 1850

MARRIED

On Thusday evening last, the 29th ultimo, by the Rev. Job Taylor, Mr. J. R. Mallory to Miss Mary C. Perry, of Panola county.

October 12, 1850

MARRIED

On Thursday, the 3d of October, instant, in this place, at the residence of her father, by Rev. Jesse M. Witt, Miss Eugenie McCown, daughter of James McCown, to Dr. N. A. Morgan.

On Thursday last evening, the 10th instant, in this county, at the residence of her father, by Rev. Job Taylor, Miss Susan Ellen Taylor, daughter of J. B. E. Taylor, to Mr. Pendleton Murrah.

OBITUARY

Died, in Marshall, on the 5th of October instant, at his residence, after six months of severe affliction, Mr. W. B. Hamments, late of Bristol, England; aged 39 years and 9 months.
The deceased was an intelligent and worthy citizen. Modest and retiring in his disposition, he was upright, cheerful, and liberal in his intercourse with the world. He was an exemplary father and husband. He has left a wife and several children to mourn his loss, rendered more afflictive from the fact that they are far from the sympathising friends of their fatherland. But we feel assured that all that can be done to alleviate their distress, will be offered by our kind citizens. They will meet with warm hearts, with tender and soothing consolations.

November 9, 1850

TO TEXAS

Wm. M. Murphy, Senator from Greene County [Ala.,] has

resigned his seat in the Legislature. He is about to remove to Texas. - Mobile Tribune.

MARRIED

On Monday evening, the 7th inst., by the Rev. Jesse Witt, Mr. William E. Miller, of Bossier Parish, La., to Miss Margaret Reed Garrison, of this county.

DIED

At his residence, in this town, on Tuesday the 5th, inst., Mr. Thomas Murphy.

November 30, 1850

DIED

At Shelbyville, Texas, on Saturday the 23d of November, Laura Josephine, daughter of Dr. L. H. and Elizabeth M. Ashcroft, age 9 months and three days. [South Carolina papers please copy.]

In this town on Saturday, 23d instant, David J. Cole, late Treasurer of this County.

January 18, 1851

MARRIED

Married on Tuesday night, 21st inst., at the residence of Mr. Joseph Mason, by Rev. Jesse Witt, Mr. G. G. Gregg, of this place, to Miss Mary Ann, daughter of Rev. T. B. Wilson, late of North Alabama.

In Caddo Parish, Louisiana, on Sunday, 12th inst., by the Rev. Jesse Burch, Mr. C. S. Croon, to Miss Margaret A. Mooring, daughter of Col. T. Mooring.

January 25, 1851

MARRIED

At "Wyalusing," the residence of Col. B. L. Holcombe, by the Rev. M. W. Staples, Gen. E. Greer, of Holly Springs, Mississippi, to Anna E., eldest of "the beautiful and accomplished sisters."
Happy pair! Long may they live, and love, and may their sea of life be without a ripple, and their sky without a cloud.
[Richmond [Va.] Enquirer and Memphis Eagle please copy.]

February 22, 1851

DIED

In this county, January 30th, 1851, after a short illness, Mrs. Sarah Ann Oglesby, wife of T. B. Oglesby, and daughter of M. C. and Sarah Connell. [The Picayune and Caddo Gazette are requested to copy.]

March 8, 1851

MARRIED

On the 4th instant, at the residence of Mrs. Ellen Carstarphen, by Rev. Job Taylor, Miss Arawhanda Jane Carstarphen to Mr. Robert G. Young, all of this county.

May 31, 1851

MARRIED

Near Marshall, on Thursday evening the 29th inst., by the Rev. J. Taylor, Mr. J. S. Alexander to Miss Margarett Elizabeth McDaniel.

June 14, 1851

OBITUARY

Died, on the 12th inst., at her residence three miles from Marshall, of apoplexy [?], Mrs. Jane Laster, aged 52 years.

[Memphis Eagle, please copy.]

July 12, 1851

MARRIED

On the 3rd of July, 1851, seven miles north-east of Dangerfield [sic] by E. G. Rogers, Esq., Mr. Robert C. Hamilton to Miss Martha E. Walker, all of Titus County.

July 26, 1851

DIED

In Bowie county, north of Boston twelve miles, on the 24th of June, Martha Keturah, infant daughter of Mary E. and Hiram A. Runnels.

THE TEXAS REPUBLICAN, MARSHALL, TEXAS

August 2, 1851

FUNERAL NOTICE

Marshall Lodge. It becomes the melancholy duty of this Lodge to announce the death of one of its devoted members. Our worthy brother, ___ Ford, departed this life on the __ day of __ last, in the __ year of his age. He was made a mason in this Lodge, in the year 18__. [Usual Masonic eulogy follows.]

August 10, 1851

MARRIED

In this county on Thursday, the 31st July, by Rev. Job Taylor, Mr. O. C. Taylor to Miss Amanda Woodley.

August 23, 1851

DIED

At the residence of his father, Rev. Jesse Witt, of Marshall, Texas, the 8th instant, Mr. Daniel Witt, aged 26 years.
Mr. Witt was a pious member of the Baptist Church, and one of the best scholars of his age. At the time of his last attack he was in Independence, at Baylor University, in which institution he has at different times filled the station of Prof. of Mathematics and Prof. of Languages. [The South Western Baptist, Marion, Alabama, will please copy.]

September 20, 1851

OBITUARY

Died, on the 8th of September, A.D. 1851, at the residence of J. F. Witherspoon, Esq., Lester Lyon, aged forty seven years.
The deceased was followed to the grave by the Masonic Brethren, who buried him with the ancient honors of their craft.

October 11, 1851

MARRIED

On the 9th of September, at Cedar Grove, White County, Tennessee, by the Rev. James Morgan, Wm. C. Woods, of Harrison County, to Miss Margaretta, daughter of Gen. J. W. Simpson.

November 1, 1851

MARRIED

At the residence of Mr. J. S. Alexander, in the vicinity of Marshall, on the 23d of October, by the Rev. Job Taylor, Mr. R. W. Hussey to Miss S. T. McDaniel.

November 8, 1851

MARRIED

In Harrison County, on Tuesday evening the 4th inst., by the Rev. Jesse Witt, Mr. J. H. Munn, of Fayette County, Texas, to Miss Frances Ann Judson Cooper, daughter of Col. Charles Cooper, of Harrison.

November 15, 1851

OBITUARY

Died, at his residence, in Marshall, at 12 o'clock M, on the 7th instant, Joseph Fields, in the 69th year of his age.

December 13, 1851

MARRIED

On Thursday the 11th inst., by Judge Patillo, Mr. Richard H. Austin, of Harrison County, Texas, to Miss Martha E. Alexander, of Maury County, Tennessee.

January 3, 1852

MARRIED

On Thursday evening last, by Rev. J. M. Griffin, Mr. I. N. Fisher, of Cherokee County, to Miss Rachael A. Wells, at the residence of her father, Col. James Wells, in this county.

DIED

On the 28th of December, 1851, Mrs. Sidney S. Middleton, consort of Mr. S. G. Middleton, of Panola County, Texas, [late of Montgomery, Alabama] age twenty-three years, nine months, and twenty-eight days.   [Montgomery [Ala.] papers will please copy.]

THE TEXAS REPUBLICAN, MARSHALL, TEXAS

January 24, 1852

OBITUARY

Died, at his residence, in Panola County, on the night of the 17th inst., of consumption, after an illness of several months, Lineus Cock, in the 46th year of his life, in the full triumph of christian faith.

Mr. Cock was born in the State of Virginia, and while a youth emigrated to the State of Tennessee, and from thence to this State. He leaves a wife and seven children to mourn his loss; he was a kind and affectionate husband, and a doting father.   [The Memphis, Tennessee, and Holly Springs, Miss., papers are requested to publish.]

William R. Rector departed this life on the 19th inst., at the Planter's Hotel in this place, after a short illness; aged forty-five years. He leaves behind many friends to lament his loss.

It becomes our painful duty to announce the death of Edward L. A. Martin, by occupation a printer, and lately connected with this office. He died a few minutes after 10 o'clock, A.M., on yesterday [December 19] of consumption, in the 23d year of his age, after a lingering and painful illness of about five months, leaving a large circle of relations and friends in this State, to mourn his untimely death. (The above notice we clip from the Palestine Advocate, which pays a merited tribute to the memory of this estimable young man. Mr. M. formerly lived in this place, and while here his conduct was in every way exemplary.)

January 31, 1852

SUICIDE

A convict in the Penitentiary of this State by the name of Cornelius Cane, committed suicide, on the 7th inst., in his cell, by hanging himself with his pocket handkerchief. He was from Leon County, and sentenced to seven years' labor, for shooting at S. Tryon, with intent to kill.

MARRIED

On the 5th day of January 1852, Mr. W. A. R. D. [sic] Ward, to Miss Permelia Hendrick, of Upshur County.

THE TEXAS REPUBLICAN, MARSHALL, TEXAS

March 13, 1852

OBITUARY

John M. Gibson Lodge of I. O. O. F. No. 13. March 8, 1852. Whereas information has been received of the demise of our true and worthy Brother, Rev. Thomas M. Brocke, who departed this life on the 11th ult., in Red River County, Texas, and thus having been called from the labors of our earthly lodge, to the enjoyment of the celestial one above, held in that house not made with hands, eternal in the Heavens... Sympathise with the widow and relatives

April 24, 1852

MARRIED

At Wyalusing, the residence of Col. B. L. Holcombe, on Wednesday evening 14th inst., by the Rev. M. W. Staples, Capt. Drury Field, of this place, to Miss Frances I. Polk, of Lagrange, Tennessee.

May 1, 1852

OBITUARY

Died, at her residence in Marshall, on the 7th ult., Mrs. Susan Witt, who had nearly completed her fifty-fourth year....She was the wife of Bishop Jesse Witt, who emigrated to this State with her husband and family, about five years since, from Bedford County, Virginia. Since her residence here, she has been engaged, with her husband, in doing good. She left behind, her husband and three sons to deplore her loss, but not as those "who have no hope."

May 15, 1852

FATAL ACCIDENT

A young man named Gordon M. Griffin, was immediately killed on the Montgomery road, on Monday last. He was riding on the fore part of his wagon, when the fore-wheels suddenly fell into a deep hole in the road, and he was thrown directly under one of the wheels, which passed entirely over his body. He lingered until Tuesday morning and died. His afflicted father was with him in his last moments, and is seemingly inconsolable for his loss. [San Antonio [?] Ledger.]

THE TEXAS REPUBLICAN, MARSHALL, TEXAS

June 12, 1852

OBITUARY

Died, in Jefferson, Texas, at the residence of Mr. S. Norris, on the 4th of June, at 11:30 o'clock, Mrs. Charlotte T. Parker, aged 70 years.

Mrs. P. was born and married in Virginia. Soon after marriage, she moved to Columbia County, Georgia. Early in the settlement of North Alabama, she moved to Limestone county; in 1831 to Mississippi; and in 1849 to Texas, with her youngest daughter. [South Western Baptist, please copy.]

June 26, 1852

MARRIED

At the residence of William N. Siglar, on Friday evening, the 11th instant, by Hon. Hardy Holman, Chief Justice, Mr. William A. Wortham to Miss Adeline E. Ashcroft.
Tyler Telegraph.

In Harrison County, on Monday evening the 21st inst., by Hon. T. A. Patillo, Mr. Seneca T. Greer to Miss Mary Price.

OBITUARY

Died at his residence in Harrison County, Texas, on the 6th inst., Col. John Mann, after an illness of about twenty-one hours. Col. Mann was a native of Kentucky, but emigrated about six years ago, with his family to this State. [Jefferson Herald will please copy.]

July 10, 1852

DIED

In Marshall, on Wednesday, the 6th inst., Mr. Howard Burnside.

MARRIED

On Wednesday evening, the 7th instant, at 4 o'clock, P.M., at the residence of D... Job Taylor, by Rev. Thomas B. Wilson, Mr. T. L. Wyatt, of Mississippi, to Miss N... E. Taylor, of Marshall, Texas.

The wedding was quite a pleasant affair and was attended by a large number. The table was about sixty feet long, tastefully arranged, and literally groaning with "good things." "Uncle Joe" was the presiding genius of the feast, and of course good humor and good feeling reigned. Among the collection were about sixty ladies -bright and blooming- whose personal and intellectual charms, vivacity and grace gave life, elegance, and beauty to the scene.

DIED

On the 6th day of July, A.D., 1852, Colonel James McCown, in the 44th year of his age.

July 24, 1852

AN UNFORTUNATE AFFAIR

We learn that on Sunday last, a shocking affair came off in Shelby County. A young man named Ballard, shot his sister-in law and a negro man, and then blew his own brains out. We understand that all the parties died instantly. We have not yet learned the cause of this lamentable occurrence.
[Nacogdoches Chronicle.]

August 21, 1852

MARRIED

On the evening of the 10th inst., at the residence of Mrs. Jane R. Kaufman, by the Rev. P. W. Warrener, Franklin B. Sexton, Esq., of San Augustine, to Miss Eliza S. Richardson, of Sabine Town, Texas.

DIED

In Harrison County, August 1st, Miriam Williams, daughter of Samuel and Sarah Williams, aged 5 years and nine months.

August 28, 1852

OBITUARY

"O Death! how couldst thou seek our pleasant bower,
And steal from it our fairest, sweetest flower!"
Died, August 9th, in the town of Marshall, Texas, at the residence of J. D. R. McHenry, Miss Eliza Ann Dunn daughter of Judge James M. Dunn, formerly of Eatontown, Georgia, but more recently of Columbus, Mississippi.
[Georgia and Mississippi papers will please copy.]

September 4, 1852

OBITUARY

Died, in Caddo Pa. on the 16th ult., at the residence of her Grandfather, E. Fortsan, Elizabeth Isidara Ann Fortsan, daughter of F. M. and F. A. Fortsan, aged 2 years, 7 months and 13 days.

THE TEXAS REPUBLICAN, MARSHALL, TEXAS

October 2, 1852

DIED

In Harrison County, Texas, on Wednesday the 8th Sept. 1852, Miss Amelia Jane Taylor, daughter of Wiley O. and Adeline E. Taylor.
The obituary will appear in our next issue.

October 9, 1852

OBITUARY

Died, in Harrison County, Texas, on Wednesday the 8th Sep. 1852, Miss Amelia Jane Taylor, daughter of Wiley O. and Adeline E. Taylor. Amelia was born in Jackson County, Alabama, 24th April, 1834.   [Nashville Christian Advocate will please copy.]

Died, in this place on the 2d inst., at the residence of S. T. Greer, of typhoid fever, Mr. Myron Rob...son, in the 24th year of his age.

Died, in this county, at the residence of Jesse Cole, Esq., on the 1st inst. Mr. Green B. Butler. [Georgia papers will please copy.]

October 16, 1852

MARRIED

In Marshall, on Tuesday evening last, by Hon. T. A. Patillo, Mr. J. B. Suddeth to Miss M. E. Stone, both of this county.

DIED

At his residence, in Marshall, on Monday last, the 11th inst., Mr. William P. Craig, aged forty one years.

Died, in Marshall, on Wednesday the 13th inst., Mr. William Shreves.

October 23, 1852

DIED

On Monday night last, the 18th instant, Miss Mary Eliza, daughter of Mrs. Eliza Carsterphen, aged 13 years.
"Leaves have their time to fall,
And flowers to wither at the north wind's breath:
And stars to set - but thou hast all,
All seasons for thine own, oh, Death!"

THE TEXAS REPUBLICAN, MARSHALL, TEXAS

Departed this life on the morning of the 22d day of October, 1852, in this place, after a long and painful illness, Henrietta, youngest child of James M. and Susan Curtis, aged 2 years and 16 days.

November 6, 1852

DIED

In this place, on the 24th of October, 6 o'clock A.M., Mr. John R. Tankersly. He was born the 17th of November, 1820.   [The Columbus [Miss.] papers will please copy.]

Died, in Marshall, on Tuesday the 2d inst., James Albert Sorell, a natve of Cahawba, Dallas Co., Alabama.
[Cahawba papers please copy.]

November 13, 1852

MURDERER

The Little Rock [Ark.] Gazette of the 27th ult., says that the man Blake H. Thompson, who murdered Mr. William Finnin, in Austin, Texas, in August last, and for whom a reward of $2,000 is offered, was in Lewisburg, Ark., on the 24th. The Gazette advises the citizens to secure him, as he is a turbulent, dangerous man.

MARRIED

In this county, on Thursday evening the 11th inst., by Rev. Mr. Steel, Mr. Thomas Bently to Mrs. Mildred Bullard. The cake was received.

OBITUARY

Died at her father's residence, in Harrison County, on the 4th inst, Mrs. Amelia C. Edmunds, wife of Mr. Z. Edmunds, of Shreveport, La., and daughter of Capt. J. and Mrs. Rebecca Perry, aged 27 years, 6 months, and 5 days.

DIED

In this county on Friday night, the 5th inst., after a sudden but painful illness, Mr. Isaac Stevens.

November 20, 1852

MARRIED

Near Henderson, Rusk County, Texas, on Wednesday the

10th inst., Mr. S. W. Hudson to Miss Mary Elizabeth Cameron, of Rusk County.

DIED

At his residence in Marshall, on Wednesday night last, the 17th inst., Mr. James M. Hudson, aged forty one years, four months and three days.

November 27, 1852

OBITUARY

Died-- At his residence near Glade Spring, Texas, on the 6th of November, 1852, Major O. F. Williams in the 44th (?) year of his age, after a lingering illness of 6 days.

He was born in Hertford County, North Carolina, and left that state in company of his father, at an early age and at an early day to locate in the unsettled region of West Tennessee, where he remained four years, when he returned to North Carolina and married a Miss Winbon, a lady to whom he has been attached from his boyhood; and shortly after moved with his wife to Fayette County, Tenn., where he spent nineteen years in contentment and happiness. He removed to Texas in 1849, and resided in Harrison County until his death.

December 4, 1852

DIED

At his residence, in this county, on the 22nd inst., of consumption, Mr. William T. Weatherby, aged ... years and 8 months.

December 11, 1852

MARRIED

In this county, on the evening of the 7th inst., at the residence of Jos. M. Taylor, Esq., by the Rev. Ward Taylor, Col. James A. Pruitt, of Cass county, to Mrs. Julia A. Blades, of Harrison.   [Huntsville, Ala., Democrat, and Florence, Ala., papers please copy.]

JOURNAL ADVERTISER, SAN AUGUSTINE

August 13, 1840

Died, at Virginia Hill, the residence of his father, in Nacogdoches County, on Friday night last at 2 o'clock p.m. [sic] the 31st of July... Thompson D. Luckett, in his 21st year, the eldest son of Col. Thomas H. and Matilda D. Luckett, natives of Fauquier County, Virginia...

February 4, 1841

CORONER'S INQUEST. On Monday evening last, an Inquest was held on the body of John M. Vanduson, late of this city... came to his death by a ball shot at him from a gun or pistol, by John Coleman, Matthew Coleman, Stephen Coleman, or Thomas Brown... Killed in this town or county.

February 25, 1841

NOTICE is hereby given for the apprehension and delivery of two Negro women, Nancy and Isabella, who broke from my custody in Sabine County... confined for alledged murder of their master, Richard Partelow.   Wm. Earl, Sheriff, Sabine County.

THE TEXAS UNION, SAN AUGUSTINE

August 25, 1849

JASPER COUNTY. B. X. Mudd vs. James Robuck, Baron De Kalb Robuck, Ezekiel Robuck and Mary Keaghey.
To the Coroner of Jasper County.
Whereas, on this the 17th day of February, 1849, B. X. Mudd the Plaitiff in this Case, has filed in the office of the Clerk of the District Court for said county, praying for a writ of publication for Baron De Kalb Robuck, who is a nonresident of the State of Texas, and also charges in his petition that the aforesaid Defendants are indebted to him in the Sum of five thousand one hundred and fifty one dollars.

ADMINISTRATOR'S NOTICE. Letters of Administration having been granted to the undersigned, by the Honorable County Court of Shelby County, at the February Term of said Court, A.D. 1849, upon the estate of Mathew Duncan, deceased - all persons having claims against said estate will present

them within the time prescriped by law, [12 months,] or they will be barred - and all persons indebted to said estate will make immediate payment.
        William M. Hewitt, Sr.
        John T. Duncan, admin.

  20 DOLLARS REWARD! Strayed or Stolen!- A Mare Colt, strayed on the 29th day of October from the town of Milam, Sabine County. B. F. Weatherred.

  LOST. The Headright Certificate granted by the Board of Land Commissioners for Shelby Co., on the 19th May, 1838, to Elizabeth Buckner, Executrix of the last will and testament of John W. Buckner, deceased, for one league and labor of land, No. 466, has been lost or mislaid - and not heard of in 90 days, application will be made to the proper authorities for a duplicate.
       Elizabeth Straw, Admx.
       Leonard Straw, Admr.
   of the Estate of John W. Buckner, dec'd.

  DIVORCE. To the Sheriff of Jasper County, greeting:
  Whereas, Mary Nancy Bennett of said County, had filed a petition in my office praying for a divorce from the bond of matrimony between petitioner and Artemus Bennett, her husband, which petition alledges and charges said Defendant with abandoning her and living in adultery with one Mrs. Smith, late of Montgomery County, of said State. And affidavit having been made that the said defendant's residence is unknown to petitioner.

  ADMINISTRATOR'S NOTICE. The undersigned having been appointed Administrators of the Estate of Catharine M. Meador, deceased, at the October Term of the Hon. County Court of Sabine County, requests all persons indebted to said Estate, to make immediate payment; all persons holding claims against said Estate, are hereby notified to present them within the time prescribed by law, or they will be barred.
       J. M. Meador,
       B. W. Meador,
   Admrs. of the Estate of C. M. Meador, decd.

  NOTICE. Dr. John S. McIteeny, [formerly of Flemingsburg, Ky.,] has permanently located in Shelbyville, Shelby county, Texas, where his sevices in the practice of the various departments of his profession are respectfully tendered. The best of medical references can be given if required. Office at the Shelbyville Drug store.

  COMMISSION, RECEIVING & FORWARDING MERCHANT. Sabine City, Texas. A. W. Canfield, having fully provided himself with large and commodious Ware houses and Cotton Sheds for storage and forwarding Cotton and Merchandize, will attend faithfully to any business entrusted to his care.

ATTORNEY AT LAW. C. L. Mann will practice at all the courts of the Fifth Judicial District. Any business confided to his care will be attended to with promptness and fideity. Address: Shelbyville, Texas.

SHELBY COUNTY. To any lawful officer of said county to execute... you are hereby commanded to summon John Vanriper... to answer the complaint of Snider Samford... S. Z. Samford. Benj. Harkness, J.P.

JASPER COUNTY. G. P. May vs. J. G. Brown. To the Sheriff of Jasper County, Greeting:
Whereas a writ of attachment has been sued out before me on the on the 31st day of January A.D. 1849, by G. P. May against J. P. Brown for seven dollars and twenty cents and Whereas the said writ has been levied on a feather bed and other articles, and whereas the said J. P. Brown has secreted himself to evade the law.
This is therefore to command you to summon said J. G. Brown by publication in the Texas Union, a paper published in San Augustine in the State of Texas to be and appear at my office in the town of Zavalla on the first Saturday in May next 1849, to answer said attachment and show cause if he has any why judgment should not be rendered against him.
Given under my hand at office in the Town of Zavalla, this 3d day of March, 1849.
J. Bradshaw, J. P., J. C., B. No. 1.

September 8, 1849

The citizens of Shelbyville on the 20th inst., for the purpose of appropriating their subscription to the cleaning out of the Sabine River, to the best advantage.

SABINE CONVENTION. The Sabine River Convention met, [Milam, September 4, 1849] according to adjournment, for the purpose of letting out the contract for clearing out said River. Present, Gen. S. G. Berry, President,
Wm. H. Tucker, R.R. Groves, H. M. Kinsey, B. J. Lewis, Norris Austin, and J. M. Burrows.
J. P. Border - sec.

THE DAILY TEXAN

January 13, 1842

Murder in Nacogdoches County. A man by the name of Thomas Sims, of Nacogdoches was killed on Saturday last, at a race track 12 miles east of that place, by a man named J. Todd.-   Red Lander, 30th December.

THE TEXAS TIMES, GALVESTON

November 6, 1842

FOR SABINE. The Steamer Mustang, will leave this place for Sabine about the 25th of November, on a trading excursion up the River. Persons having goods, who are desirous to exchange them for Cotton, would do well to make an adventure. She will remain in the river Trade during the business season. Apply to John B. Singee, Cap. or Sydnor & Street.

TELEGRAPH AND TEXAS REGISTER, HOUSTON

July 13, 1842

Northern Standard. We learn that Maj. De Morse is now on his way to Clarksville, in Red River county, with a press, type, &c., and intends to issue the first number of the Standard on the 15th inst.

August 24, 1842

Northern Standard. We learn that Major De Morse was at Clarksville on the 1st, and as his press and other printing materials were on the way from Shreveport, he expected to issue the first number of the Standard on or about the 10th inst.

THE MORNING STAR, HOUSTON

November 11, 1842

NACOGDOCHES - We are glad to learn that this ancient town is again rapidly improving. The Red Lander says, "It was in 1776 one of the most flourishing places between the Mississippi and the Rio Grande; it contained upwards of 3000 inhabitants, besides a garrison of 1800 troops. One man alone [Antonio Gil y Barbo, who built the stone house] had upwards of 10,000 head of cattle and horses, who roamed between the Neches and Sabine; his corral [cow lot] was near where Milton Garret, Esq. now resides; it was built of a wall of solid rock seven feet high, enclosing ten acres of ground, some of the remains may be seen at this time."

DEMOCRATIC TELEGRAPH AND TEXAS REGISTER, HOUSTON

February 7, 1850

LAND OFFICE BURNED. On the night of the 18th of December, the Land Office in Rusk county was broken open and the books, field notes and papers of the office burned. The citizens soon after the facts became known, assembled and appointed a committie of vigilance to detect the author or authors of the deed. Mr. W. A. Hill was charged with the crime, and on examination he was bound over to await his trial at the next term of the District Court. The Magistrate required that he should give a bond of $20,000, but a writ of Habeas Corpus was issued by the Judge, and the Court reduced it to $3,000. We learn from the Aegir of Truth, that great excitement prevails in that county in regard to this outrage. The citizens are determined to ferret out the persons who aided in destroying the records of the office.

INDEX

- A -

Aaron (slave), 47
ACCIDENTAL DEATHS, 11, 63, 66, 77, 81, 96, 112
Acosta, Theodora, 46
Adams, Anurina Ann, 68
ADAMS COUNTY, ILLINOIS, 49
Adams, Elmina, 70
Adams, Jesse, 70
Adams, Wyatt Woodruff, 21
Adeline (slave), 47
Aiguier, Ulysses, 52
Aims, Charles, 52
ALAMO, 35
Alders, Thomas, 36
Aldrich, George, 12
Alexander, A.M., 75
Alexander, Angeline, 58
Alexander, J.S., 108, 110
Alexander, Martha E., 110
Alford, Mary B., 89
Alking, Alfred, 53
Allen, Elijah, 28
Allen, Hill I., 68
Allen, Hiram, 23
Allen, Jane, 55
Allen, Mary Ann, 28
Allen, William, 55
Allison, W.C., 22
AMELIA COUNTY, VIRGINIA, 96
Anderson, C.R.B., 61
Anderson, Catherine S., 98
Anderson, Charles J., 100
Anderson, John, 75, 78, 98
Anderson, Maxfield, 105
Anderson, Minerva Eliza, 78
ANDERSON, TEXAS, 86, 99
Anderson, W.N., 68
ANGELINA STOPPING HOUSE, 18
ANGELINA RIVER, 2, 18, 29
Annis, J.R., 95
ANSON COUNTY, NORTH CAROLINA, 92
ARKADELPHIA, ARKANSAS, 95
Arnold, Hariet, 51
Arnot, J.F., 40
Ashcroft, Adeline E., 113
Ashcroft, Elizabeth M., 107
Ashcroft, L.H., 107
Ashcroft, Laura Josephine, 107
Askins, Nancy, 61
Augustus, David, 7
Austin, Miss, 22

Austin, Norris, 120
Austin, Richard H., 110
Austin, Stephen F., 34, 81
AUSTIN, TEXAS, 32, 35, 59, 83, 90, 94, 116
Avery, Alexander, 54

- B -

Bagby, Amanda, 62
Bagby, Ballard C., 62
Bagby, George H., 82, 92
Bagby, John A., 62, 72, 88, 99
Bagby, Lucy Jane, 82
Bagby, Margaret, 92
Bailey, B.S., 95
Bailey, E.W., 45
Baird, Squire M., 22
Baker, Elizabeth, 21
Baker, Lewis D., 99
Baker, T., 21
BAKERY (CLARKSVILLE), 64
Ballard, Mr., 114
Ballard, Hannah A., 49
Ballard, Harvey, 49
Barber, Elisabeth, 16
Barber, George, 16
Barber, J.C., 100
Barnett, J.C., 48
Barnett, Polly, 61
Barret, Thomas C., 42, 46
BASCOMBE COUNTY, NORTH CAROLINA, 67
Bass, Catherine, 14
Bass, Joseph R., 14
BASTROP COUNTY, TEXAS, 11
BASTROP, TEXAS, 79
Bates, Permelia L., 54
Battle, Diana C., 93
Battle, James J., 86
Battle, James W., 93
Battle, Julian D., 86
BATTLE OF SAN JACINTO, 6
BAYLOR UNIVERSITY, 109
Beatie, Mrs., 94
Beaty, Elizabeth Ann, 73
Beaty, Robert E., 73
Beauchamp, John, 7
Beauchamp, Susan, 7
Becton, J.(John) M., 28, 44
BEDFORD COUNTY, TENNESSEE, 62
BEDFORD COUNTY, VIRGINIA, 112
Bedfort, John R., 70
Bee, Bernard E., 41
Bell, William, 6
Bell, Davis, 65

Bennett, Artemus, 119
Bennett, Mary Nancy, 119
Bently, Thomas, 116
Benton, W.H., 58
BERLIN, PRUSSIA, 14
Berry, Harriet Caroline, 24, 50
Berry, John G., 24, 50
Berry, S.G., 120
BETHEL, TENNESSEE, 24
Bethune, Reverend Doctor, 90
Billingsly, Ann W., 62
Billingsly, Jesse, 62
Binsgenstorfer, Solomon, 38
Birdwell, Elijah M., 82
Birdwell, George, 11
Birdwell, M.R., 11
Birdwell, Martha, 55
Birdwell, Mary Elizabeth, 82
Birdwell, Thomas G., 13
BIRMINGHAM, ENGLAND, 105
Birmingham, P.W., 88
Bishop, David, 53
Bizzell, Paulina F., 80
Bizzell, William, 80
Black, F.H., 69
Black, John D., 53
BLACK HAWK, MISSISSIPPI, 99
Blades, F.H., 105
Blades, Julia A., 117
Blake, (Bennett), 37, 39, 40
Blake, Kozia C., 40
Blankinship (Blankenship), Nancy, 59, 60
Blanton, Francis L., 56
Bogart, Margaret Ellen, 98
Bogart, Sam, 98
BOIS D'ACRE FORK (TRINIDAD RIVER), 1
Bolin, Malcolm, 94
Bonamy, Mrs. O.V., 31
Bondies, Mr., 46
Bone, Celestia Virginia Adsette, 100
Bone, Elizabeth A., 100
Bone, John W., 100
Bonner, Cynthia, 52
BOONE COUNTY, MISSOURI, 70
Border, J.P., 120
Boren, S.H., 44
BOSSIER PARISH, LOUSIANA, 107
BOSTON LODGE, 100
Bourland, James, 76
Bourland, Martha A., 69
Bourland, Mary J., 76
Bowers, Harriet Sophronia Jane, 64
Bowers, William M., 64
Bowlin, James, 21-22
Bowlin, Jeremiah, 21-22
Bowlin, William, 22

Boyce, Dr., 82
Boyce, Sarah H., 65
Boyce, William, 65
Boyer, C.E.F., 84
Boykin, O.H., 44
Boykin, W.L., 47
Bracham, (Brackeen, Brackem), W.(William), 56, 58, 61
Bracken, James, 89
Brackney, John, 63
Bradford, Cynthia, 93
Bradford, J.F., 93
Bradley, John M., 9, 15, 19
Bradshaw, J., 120
Brandon, Merett, 55
Brantley, Sarah, 45
Brazle, Mr., 43
BRAZORIA, TEXAS, 2
BRAZOS RIVER, 43, 65
Brenan, Thomas H., 21
BRENHAM, TEXAS, 72
Brent, James, 9, 12
Brent, Sarah, 9
Bridge, James S., 90
Bridge, Katherine W., 90
Bridges, J.L., 45
Briggs, William T., 87
Brinson, Matthew, 8
BRISTOL, ENGLAND, 106
BRITTAIN, D. AND COMPANY, 23
Brocke, Thomas M., 112
BROOKLYN, NEW YORK, 90
Brower, Elizabeth B., 90
Brower, John H., 90
Brown, J.G.(P.?), 120
Brown, John L., 13
Brown, Neill, 43
Brown, Rosanna, 53
Brown, Sarah M., 69
Brown, Thomas, 118
Brown, William, 56
Browning, George W., 11
Browning, Samuel, 59
Bruton, Mary L., 46
Bryant, John T., 54
Bryarly, Thomas F., 52
Bryce, John, 103
Buckner, Elizabeth, 119
Buckner, John W., 119
BUCKSNORT, TEXAS, 65
Buford, Letitia, 17
Buford, Lucas, 60
Buford, Martha, 23
Buford, Nat M., 91
Buford, Thomas J., 23
Bullard, Mildred, 116
Bundy, Captain, 79

Bunker, Thomas C., 21
Burch, Jesse, 107
BURKESVILLE, KENTUCKY, 75
Burks, Joseph, H., 81, 88, 99
Burks, N.W., 102
Burks, Thomas C., 81
Burks, Winnifred B., 88
BURLESON COUNTY, TEXAS, 43
Burns, John H., 60
Burns, Thomas S., 65
Burnside, Howard, 113
Burroughs, James M., 18
Burrows, Harriet, 49
Burrows, J.M., 120
Burton, Martha, 11
Burton, Samuel, 105
Burton, Sarah Ann, 105
Buschmeyer, Frederika, 36
Butler, Green B., 115
Butterworth, Benjamin N., 12
Butterworth, Margaret M., 12
BUTTS COUNTY, GEORGIA, 33

- C -

CADDO PARISH, LOUISIANA, 84, 102, 107, 114
Cady, Lovett, 94
CAHAWBA, ALABAMA, 116
Caldwell, A.C., 48
Caldwell, James C., 82, 87, 91
Caldwell, Martha Ann, 87
CALHOUN, TEXAS, 2
CALIFORNIA, 29, 83
Cameron, John, 56
Cameron, Mary Elizabeth, 117
Camp, Silas W., 28
Campbell, Eton (A.), 11, 36
Campbell, F.M., 104
Campbell, G.C., 11
Campbell, George, 11
Campbell, George W., 36
Campbell, Isaac, 11
Campbell, Jno. Pryor, 24
Candell, Eliza, 53
Cane, Cornelius, 111
Canfield, A.W., 119
Cantley, A.G., 36
Carmack, Samuel, 97
Carr, James, 5
Carr, John, 69
CARROL COUNTY, MISSISSIPPI, 99
Carstarphen, Arawhanda Jane, 108
Carstarphen, Ellen, 108
Carsterphen, Eliza, 115

Carsterphen, Mary Eliza, 115
Carter, John, 63
Carter, John C., 83
Cartwright, John, 3
Cartwright, Joseph, 57
Cartwright, Matthew, 18
Carvajal, Mr., 39
Casdedine, Henry, 10
CATHOLIC CHURCH (NACOGDOCHES), 27
Catlett, H.G., 94
Caton, Mrs., 82
CEDAR GROVE, TENNESSEE, 109
CELEBRATION (4th of July), 27
Chambers, T.J., 83
Chandler, Rufus, 102
Chattfield, Mary A., 68
Cherry, Rebecca, 53
Chevaillier, Charles, 35
Childs, Abram, 21
Childs, Nancy Ann, 21
Chisum, William, 53
CHOCTAW NATION, 69, 79, 89, 92, 98
CHOCTAW TELEGRAPH, 98
Chubb, Abby, 83
Chummey, Drury, 23
CHURCH BUILDING (NACOGDOCHES CATHOLIC), 27
CHURCH OF GOD, 90
CINCINNATI, OHIO, 23
CIRCUS, 23
Clack, Martha, 76
Clampet, Arena, 59
Clark, Amos, 29, 39
Clark, Barnes, 24
Clark, Cornellia, 84
Clark, Dewitt C., 29
Clark, Ed., 102
Clark, Frank H., 97
Clark, James, 52
Clark, John T., 53
Clark, Rachel, 24
Clark, Robert, 62
Clark, Rufus K., 62
Clark, Sarah D., 64
CLARKSVILLE BAKERY, 64
CLARKSVILLE FIRE, 81- 82
CLARKSVILLE HOTEL, 67
CLARKSVILLE, TENNESSEE, 67
Clements, A.E., 74
Clemons, Elizabeth, 20
Cleveland, Benjamin, 100
Clevinger, George, 33
Clute, J.R., 48
COAHUILA AND TEXAS, 92
Coats, Daniel F., 49
Cobb, Mary Ellen, 95
Cobb, R.(Richard) T., 92, 95

Cochran, John, 80
Cock, Lineus, 111
Coffman, James, 88
Coffman, L.(Lovell), 59, 61, 74
Colbert, Malinda, 69
Cole, David J., 107
Cole, Jesse, 115
Coleman, Alexander, 8, 10
Coleman, Catherine, 8, 10
Coleman, John, 118
Coleman, Matthew, 118
Coleman, Stephen, 118
Coles, W.T.F., 69
Collins, Diana, 63
Collins, John W., 63
Collins, Nancy O., 63
Collins, S.R., 5
Collins, T.L.D., 63
Collom, Allen H., 91
COLUMBIA COUNTY, GEORGIA, 113
COLUMBIA, TEXAS, 90
COLUMBUS, TEXAS, 39
COLUMBUS, MISSISSIPPI, 114
Conn, James, 2
Connell, M.C., 108
Connell, Sarah, 108
Cooper, (A.) Eliza, 59, 60
Cooper, C.C., 57
Cooper, Calvin C., 76
Cooper, Charles, 110
Cooper, Frances Ann Judson, 110
Corker, S.W.W., 47
Corley, Samuel (P.), 52, 53, 55, 57, 58, 62, 64, 68, 72-74, 76, 78, 81, 84, 87, 89, 91, 94
Cornelius, Lucy N., 95
Cornelius, Martin, 95
Cornelius, Sarah M., 95
Cornelius, William P., 77
Cornwall, Elizabeth, 22
Cornwall, William, 22
CORSICANA, TEXAS, 78, 83
Corzine, Novaline, 17
COSHATTA BLUFFS, TEXAS, 1
COTTON SHIPPING, 1, 29, 120-121
Couch, E., 92
COURTHOUSE (NACOGDOCHES), 27, 28, 29, 39, 41
COURTLAND, ALABAMA, 67
Cozart, Hiram, 23
Crabtree, Lydia A., 58, 60
Craig, William P., 115
Crain, A.H., 38
Crain, Giles, 38
Crain, Rachel, 38
Crane, Louise, 6
Crane, P.S., 6
Cravens, John E., 89

Crawford, J., 25
Crawford, William, 6
CREEK WAR, 92
Crisp, W.M., 52
Crittenden, Eliza, 77
Crittendon, William, 82
Crockett, David, 35
Crockett, John W., 35
Crook, J. (John) H., 52, 53, 54, 59, 60
Crook, L.J., 60
Crooks, Alexander M., 93
Crooks, Benjamin, 96
Croon, C.S., 107
Crosby, William N., 94
Cross, Edward, 95
Cross, Mary Frances, 95
CROSS TIMBERS (TEXAS), 1
Crouch, A.G., 48
Crow, Enoch, 61
CUMBERLAND PRESBYTERIAN CHURCH, 79
Curl, Mary, 48
Curtis, Erwin, 53
Curtis, Henrietta, 116
Curtis, James M., 116
Curtis, Susan, 116
Cushney, William H., 35
CUSTOM HOUSE (SABINE PASS, TEXAS), 1

- D -

Daggett, E.M., 16, 45
DAGUERREOTYPES (NACOGDOCHESO, 30
Dale, Calvin, 85
Dale, Rebecca, 66
DALLAS COUNTY, ALABAMA, 116
Dalph, Katherine, 53
Daniel, Martha, 15
Daniel, Mary Ann Houston, 15
Daniel, William, 15
Daniel, William C., 97
Daniels, Margaret, 89
Darnall, Sarah, 72
Davenport, John, 23
Davenport, Thomas B., 14
DAVIDSON COUNTY, TENNESSEE, 65, 76
Davidson, Ester Annie, 86
Davidson, Hopkins, 86
Davidson, Josiah, 85
Davidson, Mary, 85
Davis, A.L., 100
Davis, Alexander M., 17
Davis, Beersheba, 20
Davis, Clay, 37
Davis, Eliza J., 53

Davis, Granville, 61
Davis, John, 2
Davis, R.W., 13
Davis, Sarah, 12
Davis, William B., 37
Davis, William P., 12
Dawson, F., 97
Dean, Edward M., 61
Dean, Mary, 61
DeBall, J.W., 49
DeCamp, Abby, 22
DeCamp, J.C., 22
DeCamp, Mary, 22
DeCamp, Stephen, 22
Deck, Sarah, 53
Deen, Lunette, 56
Deen, William G., 45
deMontbrun, Baron Armand Ducos, 80
DeMorse (?), Ann Jones, 77
DeMorse, Colonel, 41
DeMorse, Charles, 63
DeMorse, Charles Wooldridge, 63
DeMorse, Lodoika (Lodoiska) C., 63, 74
DeMorse, Major, 121
Denson, A.C., 18
Denton, Mary, 52
Dew, Matilda, 77
Dial, John, 15
Dial, Joseph, 15
Dial, N.G., 15
Dickerson, Mr., 12
Dickson, A.R., 70
Dickson, Jno. B., 100
Dickson, Miranda A., 57
Dickson, Sallie R., 100
Dickson, William P., 82
Dill, D.G., 98
Dillahunty, Charles, 89
Dillingham, James, 53
Dillingham, J.(John) A., 53, 54, 55, 57, 61
Dillingham, Nancy W., 57
Dinwiddie, J.H.B., 72
Dinwiddie, Mary Ann, 63
DISTRICT COURT (NACOGDOCHES), 28-29
DIVORCES, 7, 8, 10, 11, 14, 15, 16, 21, 119
Dixon, F., 6
Dixon, F.B., 20
Dixson, Susanna Louisa, 68
Doak, David, 86
Doak, Jane, 93
Doak, Margaret S., 101
Doak, Nelson, 93, 101
DOAKSVILLE, C.N., 98
DOCTORS, 7, 119
Dodd, Atlas, 53
Donaho, William, 62
Donington, Abby, 22

Donley, S.P., 50
Donnell, Samuel Foster, 79-80
Donoho, Mary, 64
Doom, R.C., 1
Dornstin, Joseph N., 52
Doss, Benjamin H., 70
Doss, Martha Ann, 54
Doss, Mary Malvina, 70
DOUGLASS LODGE, 44
Douglass, Nancy, 91
DOUGLASS TEMPLE OF HONOR, 48
Downing, E.(H.), 23, 32, 34, 35, 41, 50
Downs, Harriet M., 12
Downs, Lodwich D., 12
DROWNINGS, 49, 51, 81
Duffield, William C., 18
Duke, John H., 71
Duke, Reverend, 56
Duke, William, 6
Duncan, Apsilla, 16, 20
Duncan, John T., 119
Duncan, Mathew, 118
Duncan, William V., 16, 20
Dunn, Eliza Ann, 114
Dunn, James M., 114
Dupree, Mr., 24
Durfee, Charles, 71, 77
Durfee, Eliza, 71
Durham, Amanda, 79
Durst, James H., 37
Durst, John, 42
DURST'S (JOSEPH) CROSSING, 18
DUTCH REFORMED CHURCH, 22
Duty, Ann, 74
Duty (Doty?), John W., 101
Duty, Mary, 57
Duty, Philip, 57, 74
Duty, R.B., 98
Duty, Sarah Catharine, 98
Duty, William W., 91
Duvall, Mrs. M., 68
Dye, H.B., 84
Dysart, E.B., 25

- E -

Earl, W.M., 5
Earl, William, 2, 118
Eaton, B., 36
Eaton, Reverend, 83
EATONTOWN, GEORGIA, 114
Eavins, Silas, 60
Eddy, Zimri William, 14, 21
Edge, David C., 74

EDINBURGH, SCOTLAND, 39
Edmonson, R., 65
Edmunds, Amelia C., 116
Edmunds, Z., 116
EDUCATION (NACOGDOCHES), 4
Edwards, John, 17
Edwards, L.U., 17
EL PASO, TEXAS, 43
Elliot, James, 90
Elliott, A.K., 81
Ellis, A., 68
Ellis, Richard, 66
Ely, Edward B., 59
EMIGRATION, 34
ENGLAND, 105, 106
Engledow, Amanda, 6
English, John D., 9
ENTERTAINMENT, 18, 38, 47
EPIDEMICS, 44, 97
EPPERSON & WILKINS, 89
Epperson, Amanda, 81
Epperson, B.H., 81
Epperson, Cina, 81
Erwin, John, 25
Erwin, Robert, 5
Estell, Mr., 35
Eubanks, Sarah M., 10
Evans, Dr., 102
Evans, Judith M., 50
Evans, Martha, 36, 102
Evans, William, 50, 103
Everett, S.H., 3
Everitt, Stephen H., 14, 21
Eves, Emily, 19
Ewing, John M., 101
EX MATRIMONAL, 21
EXECUTION, 19
EXPEDITION, 43

- F -

FAUQUIER COUNTY, VIRGINIA, 118
FAYETTE COUNTY, TENNESSEE, 117
Featherston, Martha E., 101
Featherston, William B., 101
Fedrick, Emeline, 52
Fiedson, George, 82
Field, Dr., 102
Field, Drury, 112
Fields, J.W., 69
Fields, Joseph, 110
Fields, Washington, 63
Finley, Elizabeth E., 55
Finnin, William, 116

FIRE (CLARKSVILLE, TEXAS), 81-82
FIRE (RUSK COUNTY LAND OFFICE), 122
Fisher, I.N., 110
Fitzgerald, Mr., 44
Flatau, Louis M., 14
Fleming, P.H., 94
Fleming, W., 88
FLEMINGSBURG, KENTUCKY, 119
FLORENCE, ALABAMA, 117
FLORENCE, GEORGIA, 68
Fontaine, Edward, 32
Ford, Mr. 109
Ford, J.F., 94
Ford, John S., 18
Foreman, Margaret D., 84
Foreman, William W., 84
FORT BEND COUNTY, TEXAS, 36
Fort, Diana C., 93
FORT HOUSTON, TEXAS, 5
Fort, Josiah W., 93
FORT SMITH, ARKANSAS, 34
FORT WASHITA, C.N., 89, 92, 95
Fortsan, E., 114
Fortsan, Elizabeth Isidara Ann, 114
Fortsan, F.A., 114
Fortsan, F.M., 114
Foster, Lee, 52
Foster, Martha, 23
FOURTH OF JULY CELEBRATION, 27
Fowler, Antonia Cowles, 73
Fowler, B.C., 53, 73
Fowler, Littleton, 3, 20
Fowler, Mary A., 73
Franks, Littleberry B., 10
Freeman, Alford, 52
Freeman, Eb'r, 53
Freeman, Pamlia, 52
Freeman, Bishop, 41
FREESTONE COUNTY, TEXAS, 45
Fullerton, William W., 59
Fuqua, Joshua, 74
Fyke, A., 88

- G -

Gaffeene, (Gaffeney), William, 87-88
Gaines, Catherine, 83
Gaines, Lucy G., 96
Gaines, Robert H.(E.?), 96
Galloway, Charles A., 89
GALVESTON, TEXAS, 1, 2, 27, 36, 39, 46, 83, 121
Gamble, J.W., 80
Gann, Malinda, 36
Gardner, Charles, 52

Gardner, Thomas G., 37
Garland, Frances, 86
Garland, Josiah, 86
Garret, Milton, 122
Garrett, John C., 10
Garrett, William, 10
Garrison, John C., 78
Garrison, Margaret Reed, 107
Garrison, Thomas F., 100
Gattis, John, 87
Gattis, Lizzie, 87
George, Alfred A., 18
George, Martha A., 18
George, Presly E., 9
Gibbons, Paralee, 54
Gibbons, Pamelia Jane, 57
GIBSON COUNTY, TENNESSEE, 20
Gibson, D. H., 87
GIBSON, JOHN M., LODGE, 112
GILES COUNTY, TENNESSEE, 63, 98
Gill, Jane Chandler, 64
Gill, William H., 64
Gillet, James S., 79
Gilliam, James, 72
Gilliam, Sarah Jane, 72
Gillum, Dudley, 55
GLADE SPRING, TEXAS, 117
Gleavos, Michael, 76
Glover, Joseph, 79
Goins, Live, 56
Gooding, Henry, 75, 85
Gooding, Lemuel, 92, 95
Gooding, Mary Ellen, 92
Goodwin, Sydney B., 104
Gordon, Mrs., 64
GORDON COUNTY, GEORGIA, 90
Gordon, George, 75, 82
Gordon, George (Jr.), 75
Gordon, Isabella, 75
Gorrison, Fredrick, 46
Graham, James, 53, 64, 69
Graham, Jane, 54
Graham, Robert H., 52
GRAND ECORE, LOUISIANA, 32
GRAND LODGE OF TEXAS (MASONIC), 31
Gray, Ann, 9
Gray, Peter W., 39
GREEN COUNTY, ALABAMA, 106
Greenman, S.P., 74
Greer, E., 107
Greer, L.V., 15
Greer, S.(Seneca) T., 113, 115
Gregg, G.(George) G., 103, 107
Gregg, John, 59, 60
Gregg, Sarah D., 103
Griffin, Gordon M., 112

Griffin, J.M., 110
GRIMES COUNTY, TEXAS, 86, 99
Groves, R.R., 120
Guest, Martin, 81
Gum, Martha, 59
Guthrie, James, 82

- H -

HABERSHAM COUNTY, GEORGIA, 100
Hagan, Nellie, 23
Hagee, John W., 78
Haggerty, Jefferson, 9
Haile, John C., 20
Hale, James Randolph, 23
Hall, Miss A.E.J., 105
Hall, Amos, 12
Hall, James, 12
Hall, Samuel, 12
Haltom, Martha M., 28
Hamblin, Martha, 94
Hamilton, Caroline, 17
Hamilton, Martha P., 58
Hamilton, Robert C., 108
Hamilton, W.J., 58
Hamments, W.B., 106
Hammond, Mr., 29, 30
Hampton, Melissa, 6
Hamsley, P.J., 19
Hancock, H.C., 34
Handley, A.E., 45
HANGING (SALEDO), 44
Hankly, Henry, 18
Hanks, Horatio M., 25
Hanks, Isabella H., 25
Hanks, Minerva Ann, 52
Hanks, Peter, 25
Hansborough, Mr., 39
Harbenger, J.H., 98
Hardeman, W.B., 48
Hardin, David, 71
Harkness, Benjamin, 120
Harman, Chief Justice, 101
Harmon, Amanda, 76
Harmon, Catherine, 57
Harmon, J.(John) T., 60, 76
Harmon, Matilda, 60
Harned, Warren C., 48
Harper, Daniel E., 14
Harper, Elizabeth, 14
Harper, Elizabeth John, 79
Harper, R.H., 79
Harris, Mrs., 20
Harris, Alfred, 60

Harris, B.F., 85
Harris, Frances, 103
Harris, J.C., 106
Harris, John B., 87
Harris, Micajeh, 103
Harris, R.(Randolph) C., 60, 68
Harris, T.A., 104, 106
Harris, Theo, 13
Harrison, Mr., 42
HARRISON COUNTY, TEXAS, 4
Harrison, J.C., 34, 43
Harrison, William C., 54
Hart, Cinthia, 58
Hart, J.C., 82
Hart, James, 26, 36, 37, 45, 46, 48, 49, 51
Hart, Margaret, 90
Hart, William, 6
Harvey, William B., 2
Harvick, Sarah, 56
Hawkins, Mr., 50
Hawkins, Annie R., 97
Haynes, H.C., 90
Haynes, Mary Ann, 88
HAYS COUNTY, TEXAS, 79
Hays, Robert, 94
Hayter, A.S., 46
Heald, J.H., 90
Heald, Lucy, 90
Heard, William, 73
Heath, James, 59
Heatherly, Elizabeth, 54
Heatherly, Thomas, 65
Heatherly, Colonel, 73
HEMPSTEAD COUNTY, ARKANSAS, 95
HENDERSON, TEXAS, 32
Henderson, Governor, 43
Henderson, E.M., 85
HENDERSON FLAG, 35
Henderson, James, 61
Henderson, Josephine, 74
Henderson, L.D., 71, 72, 74, 96
Henderson, L.R., 85
Henderson, Malinda K., 71
Henderson, Maria Louise, 85
Henderson, Sarah, 72
Henderson, Thomas, 52
Henderson, Virginia, 96
Hendrick, Permelia, 111
Hendricks, Anna M.L., 96
Hendricks, Elizabeth, 12
Hendricks, John, 96
Hendricks, Mary F., 96
Hendricks, William, 12
Hennesy, R., 27
Hennise, J.J., 8
Henry, William C., 23

Herley, Sermilia, 52
Herrin, Abner, 104
HERTFORD COUNTY, NORTH CAROLINA, 117
Hervey, Mary A., 32
Hewitt, William M., 119
Hickey, West W., 65
HICKORY GROVE, MISSISSIPPI, 65
Hicks, A.W.O., 15
Hicks, Catharine, 6
Hicks, William B., 6
Highfill(?), Miss, 64
Hightower, R.S., 102
HIGHWAYS (NACOGDOCHES), 27
Hilburn, Lizie(?), 64
Hilburn, Mathias, 64
Hill, W.A., 122
Hill, Washington L., 32
Hinds, Hanson, 3
Hinds, Homer, 3
Hinds, Palafox, 3
Hobart, Mr., 30
Hobbs, Isaac, 60
Hobbs, Mary, 58, 60
Hobbs, P.W., 68
Hogan, Martha, 52
Hogan, William, 19
Hogg, Colonel, 102
Hokes, A.N., 58
Holcombe(?), Anna E., 107
Holcombe, B.L., 107, 112
Holcombe, Elizabeth Louisiana, 105
Holcombe, H.B., 105
HOLIDAYS, 27
Hollis, Jane, 34
Hollis, W., 34
HOLLY SPRINGS, MISSISSIPPI, 71, 72, 107, 111
Holman, Anne, 4
Holman, Hardy, 113
Holman, James, 32
Holman, Laura Isadora, 63
Holman, Mary B., 63
Holman, R., 63
Holman, Sandford, 12
Holmes, Cornelia Virginia, 19
Holmes, James B., 19
Holmes, O.L., 38
Holmes, Stephen, 14
Holts, P.W., 68
Hooper, Richard, 15, 17, 19
Hopkins, A.N., 55, 56, 57, 58, 60
Horne, Brent, 54
Horton, Alexander, 18
Horton, Jane D., 48
HOT SPRINGS COUNTY, ARKANSAS, 97
HOTELS, 30, 31, 32, 67, 81-82
Houndshell, Amanda C., 64

House, Littleton W., 71
HOUSTON, TEXAS, 2, 39
Houston, A., 40
Houston, President, 42
Houston, Sam, 35, 41
Howard, Alfred T., 100
Howard, Thomas B., 36
Howel (Howell), Nelson, 9, 17
Hoxey, Dr., 79
Hoxey, Sarah, 79
HUBBARDSTON, MASSACHUSETTS, 90
Hubert, Frank, 79
Hubert, Lacey G., 25
Hudgins, Thomas, 93
Hudgins, Thomas D., 80
Hudson, James M., 117
Hudson, S.W., 117
Hughes, M.A., 31
Hughes, Reverend, 89
Hunt, Benjamin F., 44
Hunt, Mrs. R., 60
Hunter, B.B.B., 105
Hunter, Carolina, 105
Hunter, Mary Myers, 5
HUNTSVILLE, ALABAMA, 58, 117
HUNTSVILLE, TEXAS, 40
Hurt, Mary L., 8
Hurt, Robert Devin, 8
Hurt, William M., 2, 8
Hussey, R.W., 110
Hutchins, Polly, 53
Hutchinson, J., 105
Hyde, G. (George) S., 7, 37, 51

- I -

INDEPENDENT ORDER OF ODD FELLOWS, 39, 47, 89, 112
INDIANS, 42
Ingram, W.C., 53
IRELAND, 69
Irish, Milton, 19

- J -

Jackson, America, 54
Jackson, Charles W., 8
JACKSON COUNTY, ALABAMA, 115
Jackson, John, 77
JAIL ESCAPES, 10, 38
James, Amelia M., 76
James, L.M., 75, 86
James, Susan M., 86

Jasper, Mary Ann, 12
Jasper, S.L.B., 12
Jasper, William, 42
JEFFERSON COUNTY, ARKANSAS, 90
Jennings, Attorney General, 36
Jett, James P., 96
Jewell, George W., 72
Jewell, Rachel, 60
Johns, Clement R., 79
Johns, David, 28
Johns, Matilda, 28
Johnson, Anna Mercer, 91
Johnson, Eliza J., 52
Johnson, James H., 91
Johnson, Lindley, 57
Johnson, Lucius, 10
Johnson, M.T., 41
Johnson, Maria C., 79
Johnson, Rebecca, 53
Johnson, Sarah Francis, 36
Johnson, T. Jeff, 6
Johnson, Thomas, 72
Johnson, William, 65
Johnson, William C., 37
Johnson, Z.C., 23
Jones (DeMorse?), Ann, 77
Jones, L., 13
Jones, Martin G., 65
JONES' PRAIRIE, TEXAS, 50
Jones, Susan, 48
JONESBOROUGH, TEXAS, 64
Jordan, Ellenor, 58
Jordan, John F., 20
Jordan, Levi, 58
Jordan, Lucy M., 68
JORDAN'S MILLS, TEXAS, 58
JOSEPH DURST'S CROSSING, 18
Joslin, Daniel, 22
Joslin, Martha C., 22
Jowers(?), Nancy, 11
Jowers(?), William G.W., 11
Juell (Jewell?), Rachel, 58, 60

- K -

KATE (STEAMER), 46
Kaufman, David S., 36, 85
Kaufman, Jane R., 36, 85, 114
KAUFMAN LODGE, 44, 46-47
Keaghey, Mary, 118
Keagrey, William S., 16
Keener, Rebecca, 94
Keith, Elizabeth, 65
Keith, James H., 73

Kelsey, H.B., 20, 102
Kemp, Johnson, 69
Kenan, Uriam T., 105
Kendal, James, 60
Kendall, Abigal B., 8
Kendall, Alman, 8
Kendall, Floyd H., 26
Kendall, Mary C., 37
Kendall, Mr., 29, 30
Kenner, Mr., 59
Kenner, Nancy, 52
Kerr, James, 80
KILLED, 9, 11, 18, 20, 24, 43, 50, 63, 75, 102, 114, 121
King, John A., 48
King, Josephine, 75
Kinsey, H.M., 120
Kirk, S.W., 47
Kirkham, William, 18
Knight, Mary J., 91
Knight, O.W., 91
KNOXVILLE, TENNESSEE, 69
Kracks, Catherine, 36
Kunolt, Ludwig, 36
Kuykendall, Sarah, 61
Kyle, R.E., 48

- L -

Laboon, Mr., 88
Laboon, Rachel, 88
Lacy, Hillary R., 11
Lacy, Martin, 11
Lacy, William K., 11
Lacy, William Y., 11
LAFAYETTE COUNTY, ARKANSAS, 98
LAGRANGE, TENNESSEE, 112
Laird, L.A.W., 56
LANANA CREEK BRIDGE (NACOGDOCHES), 33
Lancaster, Thomas A., 79
Land, Rosanna, 52
Landrum, W.L., 15
Landrum, William P., 6
Lane, John, 53
Langford, Rosetta, 59
Lanier, W.W., 13
Lapsley, Reverend Dr., 75
LAREDO, TEXAS, 70
Laster, Jane, 108
Latham, James, 5
Latimer, J.W., 68
Latimer, James, 92
Latimer, Judge, 68
Lawrence, William, 90
LAWYERS, 22, 120

Layton, Mrs., 17
Lea, Elizabeth, 74
Learza, James M., 65
LEBANNON PRESBYTERY, 79
LEBANON, TENNESSEE, 99
Lee, Mary Jane, 94
Lee, Thomas D., 83
Lee, W.D., 1
Leech, Emily, 53
Leighton, Mr., 50
LeMaird, Robert, 14
Lewis, Allison A., 3
Lewis, B.J., 120
Lewis, J.H., 94
Lewis, Mrs. L., 18
LEWISBURG, ARKANSAS, 116
LEWISVILLE, ARKANSAS, 86
LEXINGTON, KENTUCKY, 17
Lilly, Noah, 60
LIMESTONE COUNTY, ALABAMA, 92, 113
LINCOLN COUNTY, TENNESSEE, 24
LINN FLAT, TEXAS, 32
LITTLE ROCK GAZETTE, 116
Livingston, Charles, 103
Livingston, George H., 42
Lock, Francis, 20
Lockhardt, Henry, 51
Lockhart, Lucien, 17
Logan, Catharine, 11
Logan, William, 11
Look, E.(Enos) S., 57, 62
Look, Matilda, 62
Lott, E.E., 32
Lott, Mary Ann, 32
THE LOUISIANA (STEAMER), 39
LOUISVILLE, ARKANSAS, 86
LOUISVILLE, KENTUCKY, 59, 98
Love, Francis, 7
Love, George, 97
Love, John G., 7
Love, Julia, 97
Lovejoy, G.W., 64
Lovejoy, John L., 91
Lowry, W.H., 24, 50
Loyd, James, 87
Luckett, Matilda D., 118
Luckett, Thomas H., 118
Luckett, Thompson D., 118
Lucky, Dr., 43
Lynch, Elizabeth, 75
Lynch, Thomas, 75
LYNCHBURG, VIRGINIA, 85
LYNCHING (SALEDO), 44
Lyon, Lester, 109
Lyon, W.H., 34
Lysday, Jacob, 58

- Mc -

McAdams, William, 52
McAnier, Elizabeth, 56
McAnier, Mary, 56
McCary, Mrs. C., 104
McCary, Martha, 104
McCary, N.D., 104
McClure, A.E., 15
McCoral, William, 54-55
McCown, Eugenie, 106
McCown, James, 106, 114
McCullough, Ben, 40
McDaniel, James B., 33
McDaniel, Margarett Elizabeth, 108
McDaniel, Miss S.T., 110
McDermott, J.B., 73
McDermott, Josephine A., 73
McDonald, H.G., 58
McDonald, James, 46
McDONALD LODGE, 47
McDonnal, John, 78
McDonough, John, 69
McHenry, J.D.R., 114
McIteeny, John S., 119
McIver, Mary, 10
McKay, Dr., 75
McKee, John, 76
McKelvey, James, 5
McKenzie, A.H., 52
McKenzie, J.W.(P.), 57, 58, 68, 70, 71, 77, 85, 88, 96
McKinney, William, 53
McKinzie, Abner H., 52
McMahon, David, 21
McMinn, John, 56
McPherson, Elizabeth Ann, 86
McWilliams, Robert, 23

- M -

Mabane, George W., 61
Mabbitt, L.H., 20
Maddox, (N.) Nicholas, 53, 54
MADISON COUNTY, ALABAMA, 7
MADISON COUNTY, KENTUCKY, 62, 73
MAGNOLIA, TEXAS, 46
MAIL DELIVERY, 32
Majors, Eveline S., 56
Mallory, J,R., 106
Mann, C.L., 1, 120
Mann, John, 113
MANSFIELD, LOUISIANA, 47
Mansola, Clemente, 46

MARCELLINE, ILLINOIS, 49
MARION, TEXAS, 48
MARSHALL COUNTY, ALABAMA, 21, 76
MARSHALL COUNTY, MISSISSIPPI, 86
MARSHALL LODGE, 104, 109
MARSHALL REVIEW, 56
Martin, B.H., 71
Martin, Bennett H., 31
MARTIN COUNTY, NORTH CAROLINA, 60
Martin, Edward L.A., 111
Martin, Mary Jane, 71
Martin, Sarah M., 95
Martin, Mrs. Tandy K., 6
Martin, Tandy K., 6
Mason, Joseph, 107
Mason, Patsey, 55
MASONS, 6, 31, 35, 37, 42, 44-46, 66, 67, 78, 79, 82, 105, 109
Mather, Joseph, 69
MATHEWS COUNTY, VIRGINIA, 93
Matlock, C.P., 50
Matthews, Isaac, 52
Matthews, Nathan, 13
Matthiessen, U., 73
Maulding, Catharine, 97
Maulding, Presley, 97
MAURY COUNTY, TENNESSEE, 110
May, G.P., 120
Meador, B.W., 119
Meador, Catharine M., 119
Meador, J.M., 119
Meadows, Mr., 3
Means, A.B., 18
Meaux, Dr., 96
Medford, Mr., 25
MELROSE, TEXAS, 6
MEMPHIS, TENNESSEE, 35, 70, 78, 111
Merrick, William, 76
Merrill, Everly C., 57
Messenger, W.M., 32
MEXICAN GOVERNMENT, 37, 81
MIDDLE BOGGY, 34
Middleton, S.G., 110
Middleton, Sidney S., 110
MILAM LODGE MASONS, 42
MILAM, TEXAS, 2, 3, 5, 119, 120
MILITIA (COMPANY A., NACOGDOCHES), 26
Miller, D.C., 20
Miller, William E., 107
Miller, Zachariah B., 71
MILLIDGEVILLE, GEORGIA, 68
Mills, John T., 76
Mills, Judge, 79
MILLS & MURRAY LAW OFFICE, 82
Millsap, Elizabeth, 65
Millstead, John, 58
Millwee, William H., 76

MISSION (SAN AUGUSTINE), 19
MISSIONARY, 79
Mitchell, R.T., 105
Mitchell, Sarah, 91
MOBILE, ALABAMA, 105
MOBILE TRIBUNE, 107
Moffit, Mr., 4
MONTEREY, MEXICO, 70
MONTGOMERY, ALABAMA, 40, 110
Montgomery, Andrew, 16
Montgomery, John, 81, 99
Montgomery, John J., 63
Montgomery, Mary, 99
MONTGOMERY ROAD, 112
Montgomery, William T., 98
Moore, Mr., 42
Moore, E.W., 77
Moore, Gabriel H., 10
Moore (More), L.V., 59, 60, 61
Moore, Lavina, 31
Moore, Lizzie A., 46
Moore, Matthew, 10
Moore, Nickloss Y., 9
Moore, Sarah Ann, 31
Moore, Silas, 53
Moore, W.M., 31, 33
Mooring, Margaret, A., 107
Mooring, T., 107
Moreland, Isaac N., 6
Morgan, Emma, 86
Morgan, James, 109
Morgan, Joshua, 52
Morgan, N.A., 106
Morgan, S.H., 86
MORIAH CAMPGROUND, TENNESSEE(?), 67
Mork, J.W., 68
Morrill, A., 82
Morrill, Amos, 57
Morse, Charles, 8
Morse, Felix, 90
MOSELEY'S LANDING, TEXAS, 43
Mosely, Sam F., 84
MOUNT VERNON CHAPTER MASONS, 45
Muckleroy, Amanda M., 49
Muckleroy, Eliza Helen, 49
Muckleroy, Henderson, 37
Muckleroy, Jesse H., 49
Mudd, B.X., 118
Mulholland, B., 5
Mullins, Milton J., 85
Munn, J.H., 110
MURDERS, 10, 20, 24, 25, 37, 39, 44, 50,
    87, 88, 89, 94, 102, 114, 116, 118, 121
MURFREESBORO, TENNESSEE, 71
Murheh, Mr., 60
Murphy, James M., 94

Murphy, Priscilla, 16
Murphy, Thomas, 107
Murphy, Thomas G., 74
Murphy, William M., 106
Murphy (Murphey), Willis (M.), 2, 16, 25
Murrah, Pendleton, 106
Murray, J.A.N., 76, 86
MURVALL'S BAYOU, TEXAS, 17
MUSTANG (STEAMER), 121
Myers, Jemina, 88
Myers, John, 88
Myrick, H.W.K., 17
Myrick, John E., 17

- N -

NACOGDOCHES, 2, 4, 22, 26, 27, 32, 33, 38, 121, 122
NACOGDOCHES CHRONICLE, 100, 101, 114
NACOGDOCHES COUNTY, 1, 7, 121
NACOGDOCHES TIMES PROSPECTUS, 26
NACOGDOCHES UNIVERSITY, 27
Nail, Harriet, 9, 17
Nash, Cooper B., 50
Nash, Mary E., 50
NASHVILLE, TENNESSEE, 23, 57, 92
NATIONAL VINDICATOR, 72
NECHES RIVER, 122
Needham, Samuel, 2
Nelms, E., 86
Nelms, Edwina A., 86
Nelson, A.A., 17
Nelson, H., 38
Nelson, Horatio, 39
Neris, Reverend, 49
Nevill, A., 65
NEW ORLEANS, LOUISIANA, 22, 35, 39, 90
NEW YORK CITY, 22, 90
Newland, William H., 64
NEWSPAPER PROSPECTUS, 26
Newton, M.A., 47
Nicholson, John, 10
Nickerson, Thomas A., 39
Noble, Susan, 19
Noble, Thomas, 19
Norris, S., 113
NORTHERN STANDARD, 121
Norton, D.O., 58, 60
Norwood, Frances, 89
Norwood, James M., 91
Nowell, Isaac J., 53
Nunneley, W.L., 81
Nunnellee, John, 78
Nunnellee, Nancy, 78

- O -

OAK HILL, ARKANSAS, 98
Ochiltree, Miss C., 49
Ochiltree, Miss C.A., 92
Ochiltree, W.B., 49, 92
Oglesby, Sarah Ann, 108
Oglesby, T.B., 108
OLD THREE HUNDRED, 34
OLEANDER, ALABAMA, 21
Oliver, Ananias G., 13
Oliver, George W., 13
Oliver, Ingles, 64
Oliver, J.K., 68
Oliver, J.(Jefferson) W., 8, 13, 15
Oliver, Minerva Ann, 52
Oliver, Nancy, 8, 13
Oliver, Robert (F.), 8, 13
Oliver, Sarah J., 15
Orton, Mr., 28

- P -

PACIFIC RAILROAD COMPANY, 87
Padon, Dr., 90
Page, Rhoda, 60
Pairan, James, 59
PALESTINE ADVOCATE, 111
PARADISE, TEXAS, 84
Paris, William B.(D.?), 16, 20
Parker, Charlotte T., 113
Parker, Martha, 60
PARMALEE AND COMPANY, 51
Partelow, Richard, 118
Paterson, Jno. T., 2
Patillo, T.A., 110, 113, 115
Patterson, G.H., 34
Patterson, Greenville H., 34
Patterson, Sarah T., 34
Patton, A.B., 19
Patton, Napoleon, 54
Patton, W.B., 105
PATTONIA, TEXAS, 29
Payne, Buckner H., 44
Payne, Mary Hunt, 44
Payne, Mary J., 44
Payne, Rhoda, 59
Payne, Samuel, 13, 15
Peabody, Charles H., 92
Peavee, Reverend, 79
PEE DEE, TEXAS, 78
Pegues, Sarah E., 84
PENDLETON, SOUTH CAROLINA, 41

Pennall, Robert A., 21
Pennington, John E., 8
Perkins, Jane E., 13
Perkins, James, 19
Perkins, Reverend, 78
Perry, George B., 43
Perry, J., 116
Perry, Mary C., 106
Perry, Octavio E., 43
Perry, Rebecca, 116
Peters, John S., 67
Peters, Lemuel, 54, 65, 101
Peters, Richard, 73
Pevey (Peavee), Reverend, 79, 84
Phelps, Augustus, 5
PHILADELPHIA, PENNSYLVANIA, 67, 77, 83
PHOTOGRAPHS, 30
Pickett, W.M., 85
Pierce, Reverend, 79
PIKE COUNTY, GEORGIA, 24
PIND BLUFF LODGE, 45
PINE BLUFFS, TEXAS, 69, 70, 76, 94
PINE CREEK, 59, 66, 67, 88
PLANTER'S HOTEL (NACOGDOCHES), 30
PLANTER'S HOTEL (MARSHALL), 111
Polk, A.(Alfred), 17, 20
Polk, Frances I., 112
PONTOTOC, MISSISSIPPI, 74
Pope, Sarah, 53
Pope, William A., 43
Porter, Elizabeth, 3
PORTER'S BLUFFS, TEXAS, 74
Portwood, Robert, 13
Potter, Harriet, 52
Potts, Ramsey, 56
Powell, C.B., 17
Power, James M., 49
Powers, James, 32
PRESTON (STEAMBOAT), 88
PRESTON, TEXAS, 80
Price, Alfred, 12
Price, Clinton A., 5
Price, John, 36
Price, Mary, 113
Price, Sally Ann, 12
Price, Sue L., 36
Price, Susan A., 50
Pritchard, Mrs., 55
Proctor, Lucinda, 54
PROTESTANT EPISCOPAL CHURCH (NACOGDOCHES), 27, 28, 41
Provine, Reverend, 74
Pruitt, James A., 117

- Q -

Quirk, Edmond, 21
Quirk, Thomas, 21

- R -

RACE TRACK (NACOGDOCHES), 121
Ragen, Gilbert, 64
Raguet, Condy, 37
Rainey, David, 76
Rainey, Sarah, 77
Rains, Dr., 75
Ramsdall, Oliver, 83
Raney, Jane, 59
Raney, Stephen D., 70
RANKIN LODGE, 39, 47
Ratton, L. (Littleton), 59, 60
Ratton, Malinda, 60
Read, James, 96
Reagan, John H., 86
REAL ESTATE, 1-2, 21, 32
Rector, Franklin, 36
Rector, William R., 111
REDLANDER, 121, 122
Reed, John W., 54
Reeves, John P., 80
REFUGIO COUNTY, TEXAS, 32
REGULATOR-MODERATOR WAR, 4
Renfro, David, 12
Renfro, Martha, 12
REYNOLDS CIRCUS, 23
Reynolds, Lucinda H., 70
Reynolds, Reuben W., 70
Ribble, Annovanda, 80
Ribble, Catharine, 74
Richardson, Eliza S., 114
Richey, Ann G., 67
Richey, Samuel A., 67
RICHLAND, TEXAS, 68
RICHMOND, KENTUCKY, 65
RICHMOND, VIRGINIA, 66, 91
Riley, J. (James) W., 53 60
RINGWOOD, TEXAS, 64
RIO GRANDE RIVER, 37, 122
Ritchey, John M., 52
Rivers, Jones, 39
Robbson(?), Martha Maggie, 64
Robbson (?), Myron, 115
Roberts, Dr., 24, 50
Roberts, J.F., 12
Roberts, Judge, 28
Robertson, A.B.(R.?), 58, 60

Robertson, Henry, 59, 60
Robertson, Joel, 3
Robinson, Mr., 44
Robinson, James V., 51
Robuck, Baron de Kalb, 118
Robuck, Ezekiel, 118
Robuck, James, 118
Rochelle, Eugene B., 98
Rodgers, James, 55
Rogers, Barbara Braiolic, 84
Rogers, E.C., 87
Rogers, E.G., 108
Rogers, J. (James) H. (Harrison), 41, 49, 84, 92
Rogers, Mary Catherine, 87
Rogers, W.P., 39
Rohte, John C., 34
Rohte, Mr., 46
Roland, Emeline, 52
Roland, Martha, 53
ROSBOROUGH, TEXAS, 77
Rositer (Roseter, Rasiter), Samuel, 9, 17
Rountree, Montreville C., 65
Row, Mary Ann, 53
RUGGLESVILLE, C.N., 89
Runnels, Mr., 39
Runnels, Edward, 73
Runnels, Hiram A., 108
Runnels, Howell R., 84
Runnels, Martha, 73
Runnels, Martha Keturah, 108
Runnels, Mary E., 108
Runnels, Smithey Jane, 84
Runnels, Zerikia, 73
Rusk, Benjamin L., 38
RUSK COUNTY, LAND OFFICE FIRE, 122
Rusk, General, 40, 43, 101
Rusk, Mrs., 100
Rusk, T.J., 38, 87
RUSK, TEXAS, 75, 102
Rusk, Thomas J., 100
Russell, Alexander J., 74, 77
Russell, Charles W., 58
Russell, Mrs. E.A., 104
Russell, Fanny M., 55
Russell, Isabella F., 75
Russell, J.R., 93
Russell, James W., 77, 82
Russell, Mary, 70
Russell, Sarah A., 100
RUTHERFORD COUNTY, TENNESSEE, 71
Rutherford, J. (John) A., 58, 60
Rutherford, Judge, 52
Ruthven, A.S., 39
Ryder, Mary K., 70

- S -

SABINE CITY, TEXAS, 1, 119
SABINE PASS, 1, 46
SABINE RIVER, 1, 120, 121, 122
SABINE RIVER CONVENTION, 120
SABINE TOWN, TEXAS, 22, 36, 85, 114
Sach(?), Joseph, 61
SALEDO, TEXAS, 44
SALISBURY, MASSACHUSETTS, 57
Samford, S.Z., 120
Samford, Snider, 120
Sampson, J.M., 54
Sampson, James, 57, 63, 70, 71, 80
Sampson, Jane J., 52
SAN ANTONIO, TEXAS, 37, 80
SAN AUGUSTINE REDLANDER, 121, 122
SAN AUGUSTINE, TEXAS, 2, 6, 27, 35, 40
SAN JACINTO (hero of), 6
SAN MARCOS, TEXAS, 79
Sanford, Simon Z., 45
Sansom, Reverend, 27
SANTA ROSA, MEXICO, 29
Saufley, William P., 77
SAVANNAH, TEXAS, 57, 62, 65, 69
Schoolcraft, Susan, 60
SCHOOLS (NACOGDOCHES), 4
Schoonover, Elizabeth, 53
Schoonover, Harrietta, 53
Schroeder, Henry, 36
SCOTLAND, 39
Scott, Martha A., 39
Seeton, J.M., 48
Settle, Marcus G., 70
SEVIER COUNTY, ARKANSAS, 61, 78, 80, 81
Sexton, Franklin B., 114
Shanks, A.H., 105
Shanks, Lavinia, 20
Sharkey, Mrs., 99
Sharkey, Greenwood L., 99
Sharp, James M., 61
Sharp, Mr., 40
Shelby, Alfred I., 21
SHELBY COUNTY, TENNESSEE, 57
SHELBY COUNTY, TEXAS, 4, 114, 120
SHELBYVILLE, TEXAS, 21, 119, 120
Shepert, John G., 53
Shepherd, Simpson, 37
Shook, J., 61
SHOOTINGS, 3, 9, 18, 24, 43, 50, 102, 114, 118
SHREVEPORT, LOUISIANA, 80, 94, 116, 121
Shreves, William, 115
Shryock, Madison H., 13
Siglar, William N., 113
Simmons, Isabella, 68

Simmons, Joseph, 19
Simpson, Francis A., 37
Simpson, Miss J.C., 17
Simpson, J.W., 109
Simpson, John J., 37
Simpson, Major, 41
Simpson, Margaretta, 109
Simpson, Tabitha R., 50
Simpson, Victor J., 51
Simpson, William M., 17
Simpson, William P., 50
Sims, Alfred G., 45
Sims, J.W., 69
Sims, Mary, 11
Sims, Mary Julia, 69
Sims, Susan L., 69
Sims, Thomas, 121
Sims, William, 11
Sinclair, Malcolm, 24
Sinclair, Samuel, 94
Singee, John B., 121
SISTERVILLE, TENNESSEE, 67
Skidmore, Eliza Ann, 53
Skiles, Harvey, 60
Slaughter, Hannah A.G., 14
Slaughter, John Calvin, 14
Slaughter, Nancy, 18
Slaughter, S.M., 2
Slaughter, William H., 14
Slayton, George W., 97
Smith, Mr., 43
Smith, Mrs., 119
Smith, Angeline, 53
Smith, Freemon, 67
Smith, Henry, 72
Smith, James A., 91
Smith, James N., 54
Smith, Joseph, J., 70
Smith, Josiah, 100
Smith, Lafayette, 89
Smith, Louisa, 74
Smith, Martha, 67
Smith, Martha Ann, 54, 55
Smith, Mary G., 98
Smith, Morgan L., 90
Smith, Nathaniel, 5
Smith, P., 72
Smith, Samuel S.(Simpson), 66, 67
Smith, Thomas, 50
SMITHFIELD, TEXAS, 1
SMITHLAND, TEXAS, 94
Snelser, James B., 83
Snow, Lewis M., 53
SONORA, CALIFORNIA, 83
SONS OF TEMPERANCE, 32, 39, 73
Sorell, James Albert, 116

SOUTHWESTERN BAPTIST, 109, 113
Sparks, Andrew J., 28
Spears, Thomas, 59
Speer, Moses, 3
Speight, W.D.R., 1
Spelling, William, 74
Sprole, Reverend Mr., 19
ST. CLAIR COUNTY, ILLINOIS, 61, 75
ST. LANDRY, LOUISIANA, 21
ST. LUKE'S CHURCH (PHILADELPHIA), 77
Staats, Nelson, 57
STABBINGS, 20, 50
STAGE COACH\STAGE LINES, 32, 40, 51
Stallings, Abraham, 54
Stanfield, Sarah, 22
Stanfield, William, 22
Staples, M.W., 107, 112
STAR HOTEL (CLARKSVILLE), 81-82
STAR STATE PATRIOT, 84
Starkey, Elizabeth, 75
Starkey, John, 61
Starnes, Aaron, 58
Starnes, Susan, 58
STEAMBOATS, 1, 2, 29, 39, 46, 88, 96, 121
Steel, Reverend, 116
Steel, William, 104
Stephen, Mr., 93
Stephenson, James, 90
Stevens, Isaac, 116
Steward, Mary Jane, 48
Stewart, Catherine W., 65
Stewart, Hugh M., 100
Stewart, John, 3
Stewart, Margaret A., 65
Stivers, Eliza Jane, 9
Stivers, Samuel, 9
Stockton, Emma, 77
Stockton, William T., 77
STONE HOUSE (NACOGDOCHES), 22, 122
Stone, Miss M.E., 115
Stook, Nathan, 76
Story, Ephraim, 9, 17
Stout, Mary Helen, 62
Stout, Matilda C., 62
Stout, Sarah Isabella, 62
Stout, Susan Elizabeth, 78
Stout, William B., 59, 61, 62, 78
Stowe, H. (Harriet) B. (Beecher), 47
Stowell, Willard, 52
Straw, Elizabeth, 119
Straw, Leonard, 119
Strawn, James W., 68
STREETS (NACOGDOCHES), 27, 33
Stricklin, Bolin, 86
Stricklin, Jane M., 86
Strode, Emily, 49

Strother, Sarah E., 101
Strother, William, 101
Stroud, Iraanna W., 104
Stroud, Minerva A., 104
Suddeth, J.B., 115
SUICIDES, 40, 65, 78, 111
SULPHER BOTTOM, 77
SULPHER SPRINGS (NATURAL), 2
SUNDAY SCHOOL (NACOGDOCHES), 38
SUPPORT (SPOUSAL), 11
SURVEYOR, 1
Suttonfield, Frances, 74
Swan, S.G., 89
Swanson, Odessa F., 69
Swearingin, A.C., 9
SWITZERLAND, 38
SYDNOR & STREET, 121

- T -

Tabor, James, 10
Talbot, Letitia E., 75
Taliaferro, Eliza Isabella, 21
Taliaferro, Nicholas J., 7
Tankersly, John R., 116
Tarrant, General, 42
Taylor, Adeline E., 115
Taylor, Amelia Jane, 115
Taylor, J.B.E., 106
Taylor, Job, 106, 108, 109, 110, 113
Taylor, Joseph M., 105, 117
Taylor, Julia A., 105
Taylor, Miss N.E., 113
Taylor, Nancy, 61
Taylor, O.C., 109
Taylor, Susan Ellen, 106
Taylor, Ward, 117
Taylor, Wiley O., 115
TENEHAW GANG, 4
Terrell, General, 42
TEXAS (REPUBLIC) CONGRESS, 32, 81
Thacker, Nancy, 25
THEATRE ROYAL, 55
Thom, John, 73
Thomas, Joseph M., 53
Thomas, Mary Ann, 24
Thomas, Mary J., 32
Thomas, Susan A., 77
Thomas, William M., 84
Thompson, Abner W., 79
Thompson, Blake H., 116
Thompson, E. (Edward), 59, 60
Thompson, Henry S., 17
Thompson, John P., 102

Thompson, Lucretia, 59, 60
Thompson, Margaret F., 17
Thompson, Samuel, 2
Thomson, Frank, 99
Thomson, William Hatten, 87
Thorn, Frost, 25, 31
Tinnin, Mary Ann, 78
Tinnin, Sarah, 76
Tinnin, William, 76, 78
Titus, James, 57, 65
Titus, Rebecca, 65
Titus, T.F., 69
Todd, Ada S., 94
Todd, Eliza A., 76, 93
Todd, J., 121
Todd, James D., 94
Todd, William, 25
Todd, William G., 76
Todd, William S., 76, 83, 93
Tohlen, Margaretta, 36
Tomlinson, J.W., 57
TOURISM (NACOGDOCHES), 31-32
TREATY OAK (TARRANT COUNTY), 42
TRENTON, TENNESSEE, 20
TRIMBLE & HUDGINS, 81-82
Trimble, Buena Vista, 70
Trimble, Henry, 54
Trimble, Lucetta, 70
Trimble, William, 70, 85
TRINIDAD RIVER, 1
TRINITY COLONY, 59
TRINITY RIVER, 1, 46
TRINITY (UPPER), 41
Tryon, S., 111
Tucker, George, 50
Tucker, James, 15
Tucker, R.R., 84
Tucker, William H., 120
Turner, Mr., 11
Turner, Charles, 18
Turner, Martha, 60
Turner, Mary, 52
Turner, Ruffin, 2
Turner, Sarah, 52, 58
Tutt, James, 19
Tuttle, Mr., 96
TYLER TELEGRAPH, 113

- U -

UNCLE TOM'S CABIN, 47
UNION DISTRICT, SOUTH CAROLINA, 87
UNION SUNDAY SCHOOL (NACOGDOCHES), 38
UNIONVILLE, TEXAS, 90

Ury, Amos, 95
Ury, George, 95

- V -

Vanduson, John M., 118
VanDyke, L.D., 58
Vann, Jane, 7
Vann, Mason M., 7
Vanriper, John, 120
Vaught, Andrew, 52
Vaught, Montgomery, 52
Vining, John Johns, 58
Vining, Martha, 70
Vining, Thomas L., 83
Vining, Wade H.(Hampton), 70, 83, 92
Vining, William W., 70
VIRGINIA HILL, TEXAS, 118
Voigt, Henry, 36

- W -

Wagley, Simon, 55
Walding, Greenbery, 56
Waldrop, Claborn, 22
Waldrop, Polly, 22
Walker, Reverend Dr., 93
WALKER COUNTY, TEXAS, 50
Walker, Martha E., 108
Walker, Martin A., 17
Walker, Nancy, 9
Walker, Phillip, 17
Walker, Richard (Dick) S., 35
Wall, Matilda, 13
Wallace, William, 5
Waller, Mr., 12
Waller, Abner S., 13
Waller, Benjamin E., 16
Walling, James, 6
Walling, Lucinda, 6
Walling, Van, 24
Wallis, Eliza, 99
Wallis, Ezekiel, 99
Wallis, Sally, 99
WALTOOGA HALL, 74
Ward, Elizabeth, 89
Ward, James J., 72
Ward, L.(Loudon) B., 44, 48
Ward, Mary D., 72
Ward, Mat, 89
Ward, Sarah C., 65
Ward, W.A.R.D., 111

Ward, William, 89
Ware, Nancy A., 81
Ware, Ulysses H., 78
Warfield, Charles A., 58
WARREN COUNTY, MISSISSIPPI, 65
Warren, John, 16
Warren, Nancy, 16
WARREN, TEXAS, 93
Warrener (Wartener), P.W., 22, 114
Warrins, R.V., 47
Washburn, D., 77
WASHINGTON, ARKANSAS, 63, 96
Washington, Catharine H., 90
WASHINGTON COUNTY, ALABAMA, 102
WASHINGTON-ON-THE-BRAZOS, 39, 79
Waskum, John M., 97
Watkins, Lewis, 3
Watson, Cornelia, 16
Watson, Dexter, 16
Watson, Henry D., 16
Watson(?), Howell, 15
Watson, Ordera, 10
WAXAHATCHIE, TEXAS, 87
WEATHER (NACOGDOCHES), 28, 29
Weatherby, William T., 117
Weatherred, B.F., 119
Weaver, William, 48
Webb, Anderson, 11
Webb, Joel D., 68
Webb, Ruannear(?), 11
Webbs, Reverend, 65
WEDDING CELEBRATIONS, 38, 47, 64, 113
Welch, Cynthia, 75
Welch, Elizabeth, 76
Welch, James, 76
Welch, William, 75
Wells, Albert, 49
Wells, Annie V., 101
Wells, Isaiah, W., 76
Wells, James, 110
Wells, James S., 101
Wells, Lewis S., 101
Wells, Martha, 55
Wells, R.B., 29
Wells, Rachael A., 110
West, Adelia F., 58
West, Arabella, 77
West, Edward, 58, 63, 77
West, John W., 85
West, Sarah, 85
Wharton, Clement L., 13
Wheat, John, 65
Whipple, J.W., 79
Whitaker, Mr., 31
Whitaker, America, 31
Whitaker, B.F., 29

Whitaker, Nancy E., 29
Whitaker, Sarah, 56
Whitaker, Wilis, 56
WHITE COUNTY, TENNESSEE, 109
White, James D., 43
White, James T., 50
White, Josiah, 15
White, Rebecca, 43
White, Susannah N., 50
White, William, 11
Whorton, Margaret, 55
Wideman, Thomas, 53
Wiggins, R.R., 23
WILDEY LODGE, PARIS, TEXAS, 89
Wilkins, J.P.P., 31
Wilkins, John, 89
Wilkins, Sarah Caroline, 57
Wilkinson, Eliza G., 84
Wilkinson, Seaborn J., 84
WILKS COUNTY, GEORGIA, 83, 88
Williams, Ann E., 91
Williams, Ephraim, 54
Williams, Isaac M., 22
Williams, J.J., 99
Williams, James, 52
Williams, John, 104
Williams, Joseph, 91
Williams, Miriam, 114
Williams, Nancy J., 53
Williams, O.F., 117
Williams, Reuben, 61
Williams, S.W., 102
Williams, Samuel, 114
Williams, Sarah, 114
Williams, Sterling E., 52
Williams, Swain, 21
WILLIAMSON COUNTY, TEXAS, 97
Willingham, Edward, 25
Willingham, Sarah F., 25
Willingham, T. (Thomas), 24, 50-51
Willison, George, 53
Willison, Mary Ann, 100
Willison, Thomas, 52, 54, 56, 57, 59, 65, 100
Wilson, Betty, 13
WILSON COUNTY, TENNESSEE, 67
Wilson, Eliza, 19
Wilson, Jacob, 60
Wilson, Jefferson, 13
Wilson, Louisa, 52
Wilson, Mary Ann, 107
Wilson, Thomas B., 107, 113
Wilson, Thomas R., 82
Wimberly, James, 58
Winbon, Miss, 117
Windham, John L., 33
Wingfield, W.W., 17

Winkler, Clinton W., 74
Winn, James A., 10
Winn, Quean Elizabeth, 10
WIRT & WICKHAM, 66
Witherspoon, A.N., 84
Witherspoon, J.F., 109
Witherspoon, J.L., 95
Witherspoon, Martha, 54
Witt, Daniel, 109
Witt, Jesse (A.) (M.), 101, 106, 107, 109, 110, 112
Witt, Susan, 112
Wood, David R., 58, 60
Woodley, Amanda, 109
Woods, William C., 109
Woodward, A.B., 29
Woolam, J. (John) C., 28, 31
Wooldridge, John R., 83
Wooldridge, Sarah, 83
Woolton (Wootten), G.H., 77
Wooten, Joel A., 83
Wootten, Ann E., 68
Wootten (Woolton), G.H., 68
Wootten, Lemuel, 68
Wortham, Elisabeth P., 61
Wortham, Timothy, 88
Wortham, William A., 113
Wortman, Henry E., 16
Wortman, Rosanna, 16
Wright, Pleasant, 36
"Wyalusing," 107, 112
Wyatt, T.L., 113
Wyche, William P., 5
Wynn, William H., 65

- Y -

Yates, Elizabeth, 3
Yates, Joseph C., 3
Yates, Thomas, 18
YAZOO RIVER, 99
YBarbo, Antonio Gil, 122
Young, Electia Angelina, 61
Young, Hugh F., 58, 61, 77, 80
Young, Robert G., 108
Young, Sophia T., 76
Young, W.C., 76

- Z -

ZAVAL(L)A, TEXAS, 2

www.ingramcontent.com/pod-product-compliance
Lightning Source LLC
Chambersburg PA
CBHW020653300426
44112CB00007B/356